All Glorious Within

By Jean Vowell

The king's daughter is all glorious within:

her clothing is of wrought gold.

Psalm 45:13

All Glorious Within

By Jean Vowell

Chapter 1: Is God the Problem?

I HAD FALLEN INTO A RAGING STORM of loss, pain, rejection, and hopelessness. I was DEPRESSED and DRAINED; I had to QUIT my JOB because of panic attacks. With very few exceptions, I stayed inside my house for FIVE YEARS. My life was on hold because I was trying to live without the BIBLE and without FAITH.

Why? People had convinced me God wasn't any good and that He wouldn't help me.

Those people didn't expect faith to actually accomplish anything. For them, a religious mindset had replaced biblical faith in God. They insisted God was Sovereign and that He did exactly as He pleased. He might bless or curse on any given day!

Yes, they taught that Jesus was very kind, and He had died for our sins. We would go to heaven when we died. But while we lived, we would have to suffer through every problem that came into our lives.

I reasoned that God had sent such anxiety into my life because of my SIN. I thought DEPRESSION, PANIC ATTACKS, FLASHBACKS, AND HOPELESSNESS were GOD'S WILL for my life. Even though I had repented and accepted Jesus, I thought God was still holding a grudge.

Beyond believing for salvation, my faith couldn't seem to work. There were so many things I didn't understand. I wasn't sure whether God cared about my personal problems or not. Sometimes, He seemed to be my problem! Why didn't He do something to help me? I needed so much help! But He wasn't the problem. I was! Most of my ideas about God were wrong.

I needed to view God differently, through His own lens and not through mine. In order to perceive Him correctly, I had to learn and believe what He says about Himself. He is always good! For me, that lesson came unexpectedly.

One day I whispered a desperate prayer. I said, "God, help me!" I was alone and afraid.

A moment later, the atmosphere in my little house changed when the presence of Jesus Christ suddenly flooded my little room. He revealed Himself to me in a powerful and gracious way and my fears were shoved over to the side.

I was conscious of nothing at that moment except His love, His power, and His goodness! He was going to help me! Yes, He is GOOD!

I instantly realized that fear, sickness, weakness, and worry had nothing to do with Him. Panic and terror had bound me for a long time, but I knew He would help me eliminate them from my life completely.

He revealed a way, and that way included practical steps. One thing I had to do was turn my back on fear! (Repenting of fear in that environment made me feel self-conscious!)

Fear had always seemed such a natural part of my life, yet His presence caused me to realize that fear is totally unnatural for a Christian. Fear is an opposite of love, and God is love!

Many things I had been taught about God were not right. Don't let incorrect ideas limit you!

Turn from things that cannot help you and turn to things that can help you! Turn from your own way to God!

That day, I took my first steps towards freedom and away from fear. I went on my porch. Yes, God answers prayer, but first He helps us believe.

Focus on peace and wholeness and expect Him to get you there! He will encourage you! He will heal you. Jesus will be with you, He will help you, and He will give you power to overcome your fears! You can learn to overcome evil with good.

That very day, I sat outside for 15 minutes. The next day, I walked a mile.

Living by Faith

"Before anything else existed, there was Christ with God. He has always been alive and is Himself God." (John 1:1 TLB)

Jesus Christ is God (Titus 2:13), He is Savior, and He invites us to "have faith in God." (Mark 11:22)

To live by FAITH is to have confidence that God's word is true and to trust it more than you trust your own feelings or your own knowledge. When problems come up, let His word show you how to deal with them. That is what you must learn to do.

Would it be honest for Jesus to say "Have faith in God" if God did not answer prayers? No, it would not be honest.

But how does God decide which prayers to answer? Since God is the absolute King, is He bound by His own word? Is God changeable? Does He alter His own promises at will? Some people think He does.

What limits Him? Only one thing can: His own word! Some people believe God is not bound by His word and that He acts contrary to His word any time He wants, moving in "mysterious ways."

Like I used to, they see God as the problem.

Your Life

Living by faith will not make your life perfect. You will still deal with problems; the difference is that you will be alive spiritually.

Living by faith will not make your life perfect. You will still deal with problems; the difference is that you will be alive spiritually. You will learn to rely on God's love, God's promises, and God's wisdom every day. He is a good Father!

The Bible has many things to say about cause and effect; it warns us about what not to do. If you choose not to let His word teach you, God WILL allow you to learn from your own mistakes.

Proverbs 3:13 (AMPC) says, "Happy (blessed, fortunate, enviable) is the man who finds skillful and godly Wisdom, and the man who gets understanding [drawing it forth from God's Word and life's experiences]." How does God teach through experiences?

Well, every situation in life is not covered in the Bible. For instance, the Bible will not tell you which college to choose. It will tell you that God has a plan for your life and that He will lead you in making choices.

Psalm 119:7 tells us we can learn to make righteous judgments. "I will praise thee with uprightness of heart, when I shall have learned thy righteous judgments."

The entire text of Psalm 119 is devoted to revealing the power of God's word. Yes, you WILL go on making mistakes and getting off track from time to time until you bring your thinking in line with God's wisdom and direction.

Don't condemn yourself if your life is not perfect. It never will be! Keep going! Keep learning. Keep having faith!

Stop trying to live a designer life. Do your best every day. That's it! Forget trying to make your life perfect for God. He already has His sleeves rolled up and He is ready to work on your spiritual makeover!

Putting your faith in God does not mean your life will be PERFECT overnight. Faith will not take you out of this fallen world.

What is God Like?

Preachers have often presented God as powerful but strange and unpredictable. They say, "You can never tell what God is going to do?" Is that true? Is He really so strange? What has He revealed about Himself?

• He is good.	Psalm 84:11, 143:10
• He cannot lie.	Num. 23:19, Titus 1:2
• He keeps His promises.	Deut. 7:9, I Cor. 1:9
• He loves us.	John 3:16, Romans 5:8
• Jesus is His express image.	Col. 1:15-17, Heb. 1:3

We have been created to be like Him. We can love because He loves; we can walk in the light because He is light. Jesus came into the world to reveal God's love, God's truth, and God's Fatherhood. His New Covenant is a fulfillment of all God's Old Covenant promises with many more promises added.

Did God Change?

Why does God seem different in the Old Testament than He does in the New Testament? In the New Testament God presents a complete revelation of His love for us through the life, ministry, redemptive death, and resurrection of Jesus Christ! In the Old Testament God could only deal with His people as servants because they were not born again. The Israelites served God; they did not know Him as Father.

If you want to see exactly what God is like, look at the life of Jesus!

Jesus said, "I came so they can have real and eternal life, more and better life than they ever dreamed of." (John 10:10 MSG)

What about sin? Jesus came and died so we could have life! He took SIN to Himself to get it out of your way and He longs to establish His covenant of love in your life.

Psalm 86:10 speaks of God's compassion. "But thou, O Lord, art a God full of compassion, and gracious, long suffering, and plenteous in mercy and truth."

Psalm 111:4 says, "He hath made his wonderful works to be remembered: the LORD is gracious and full of compassion."

Matthew 14:14 says, "And Jesus went forth, and saw a great multitude, and was moved with compassion toward them, and he healed their sick."

We see that God is full of compassion and that compassion moved Jesus to act.

Since the time I was a small child, I had been carefully taught from the Bible. Granny told me it was my duty to read it and believe it.

Others taught me too. They presented the Bible as a book of history, a book of heroes, and a book of rules. When I earnestly began to read the Bible for help, my perception of God became clearer. I learned He is Someone to trust, Someone to lean on, and Someone to learn from. He is…Good! I saw that the Bible contained answers I desperately needed. It became my spiritual food and water; it became a roadmap that would eventually lead me out of my difficulties.

God's Creation is Good

The Bible says everything God created is good. "And God saw everything that he had made, and behold, it was very good. And the evening and the morning were the sixth day." (Genesis 1:31)

Many people today believe everything that happens in life must be God's will. That is human reasoning.

Human reasoning says that if God has created everything, then He made sickness, trouble, poverty, war, and death. Terrible things came into the world when Adam gave away his dominion over it. The rulership God had given Adam then belonged to Satan.

Many see God as picky. They believe God is always choosing whether to do good things or bad. Does God hurt people? No! God's business is healing. Does He kill people? No! His business is life. Does He make people needy? No! His business is blessing people!

Does God Really Heal Today?

God wants you to be blessed and to be well. When you study His word, you see that health is a priority:

- He gave the Israelites a choice: life or death. (Deuteronomy 27)
- He lists His blessings first in Deuteronomy 28.
- He heals the brokenhearted and binds up their wounds. (Ps 147:3)
- A Redeemer was promised from the beginning. (Isa. 53:4-6)
- Jesus went about healing when He was on earth. (Acts 10:38)
- He is touched by the feelings of our infirmities. (Hebrews 4:15)

- The prayer of faith shall save the sick. (James 5:15)

God is Not Angry

The enemy will twist God's word in order to deceive; he twisted God's word when he tempted Eve. She actually had dominion over Satan at that moment, but she did not use it!

The devil will try to convince YOU that GOD has caused YOUR problems. He may even say that God is mad at you and will never forgive you. Take positive action by getting rid of all those thoughts!

The Bible says believers have the power to cast down imaginations and bring every thought into captivity to Christ. You can take authority over the devil using Jesus' name.

God is all about forgiveness, health, and growth. His plan is for you to get well, to stay well, and to grow up in Christ. Don't feel condemned if you make a mistake. God will forgive and forget mistakes as soon as you confess them.

Jesus forgave many different people, including:

- Woman taken in adultery

  John 8:3-11

- Paralyzed man

  Mark 2:1-12

- Woman at the well

  John 4:1-26

- Peter, who denied Him

  Mat. 26:74 (AMP)

- Paul (Saul), who put Christians in prison

  Acts 8:3

- Those who crucified Him

  Luke 23:34

Walk in His word every day; He will protect you. Put yourself under His giant "umbrella of protection." God's grand design is salvation for all who call on the name of the Lord Jesus! He wants us to receive good things He has promised in His word.

God's Umbrella

God has an enormous "umbrella of protection" called "the New Covenant." He calls everyone to get under that umbrella with Him so He can protect them.

Some people come under it, and some people don't. He has given each person free choice.

God welcomes everyone to come under His umbrella of covenant protection. Those who DO, enjoy all the blessings He has provided. Those who do not are still subject to the world's ups and downs.

Is that God's fault? No. He gives everyone a choice.

Stand confidently under God's umbrella! Give the Bible a place of importance in your life. Choose Jesus as your Savior. Rely directly on God for your needs.

A Burn Victim

Painful memories, guilt, shame, rejection, and trauma have destroyed many lives. You may feel like a burn victim waiting to heal; every contact with people seems to cause more pain.

A burn victim doesn't want to have contact with anyone. Maybe you feel that way now. How long will it take before you are well?

God is so much bigger than your pain! Go directly to God! It is Jesus Who heals the brokenhearted! He is the One Who sets the oppressed free!

In Luke 4:18 (MSG) Jesus says:

"God's Spirit is on Me; He's chosen Me to preach the Message of good news to the poor, sent Me to announce PARDON to prisoners and RECOVERY OF SIGHT to the blind, to set the burdened and battered FREE, to announce, 'This is God's time to shine!'"

The Spirit of Your Mind

Be renewed in the spirit of your mind! Change your attitude! See God in a new way. See yourself in a new way. See yourself as His child.

You need a system of believing and Someone to believe in; you don't need to rely on subjective reasoning based on your own experiences.

Pursue peace! Stay away from people whose lives are full of confusion and strife. Don't allow them to hurt you because it is easy for hurt to turn into bitterness. Only the carefully guarded heart can manage to avoid it. Offense is failure to forgive, and it will cause your life to go off in the wrong direction. It will also twist the way you see things. To be renewed in your mind is to see through God's lens. Your first thought should be to forgive.

Teachable

Allow the word of God to teach you. One of the most important things you can do is apply the Bible's wisdom to everyday life.

James 1:21 says, "receive with meekness the engrafted word, which is able to save your souls." The Greek word translated "meekness" means "mildness, gentleness."

A meek person is teachable, not stubborn. The only way you can truly receive the word of God is to remain meek and focus on it. If you truly desire change, focus on the word of God closely.

Jesus said: "You are truly my disciples if you live as I tell you to;
and you will know the truth, and the truth will set you free." (John 8: 31-32 TLB) Stay meek and remain teachable!
Psalm 100:4 (MSG) tells us how to come to God: "Enter with the password: 'Thank you!' Make yourselves at home, talking praise. Thank him. Worship him." Thank God for every good thing large and small. This is how you draw near; this is how you live in His presence. Praising God will release great power in your life! The more you praise, the freer you will become!
If you are born again, you are righteous. God wants you to tell Him your worries. You are His child; He loves to hear your voice talking to Him and praising Him. He invites you to enter into His presence.

There are several things to remember:

- God is not your problem.
- He has given you the ultimate solution: Jesus.
- Emotional pain does not come from God.

- God is a Healer. He wants you set free, healed, and restored!

If you truly want to know about God, go directly to Him. Don't depend on what others tell you about Him; find out for yourself!

John 14:21 (AMP) says, "The person who has My commandments and keeps them is the one who [really] loves Me; and whoever [really] loves Me will be loved by My Father, and I will love him and reveal Myself to him [I will make Myself real to him]."

"The Lord lift up His countenance upon you and give you peace." (Numbers 6:26) To "lift up the countenance" is an idiom that means "to smile."

The Lord will smile on you when you commit yourself to Jesus Christ, His Son. At the same time the Holy Spirit, your heavenly umpire, will declare you "safe." Stay close to God! Jesus died to bring you close!

For me, freedom meant much more than getting out of my house. Real, true freedom required spiritual restoration.

A Plan for Recovery

On that day I opened my Bible and discovered a verse. Obeying that verse was my first step away from crippling depression. Then I discovered another verse, and then several more. Those verses eventually formed the outline for this book!

God has provided many wonderful things in His word to help you! It is up to you to read the Bible, think about it, and draw healing from it. Fear not, little flock; for it is your Father's good pleasure to give you the kingdom. (Luke 12:32)

Your thoughts can be renewed. Your heart can become glorious with His light! The ball is now in your court!

Remember:

Stop thinking your problems are God's fault. Stop believing God doesn't care! He loves you more than you can imagine, and He wants to help you!

Chapter 2: God's Wisdom

Proverbs 2:6 (TLB) - For the Lord grants wisdom! His every word is a treasure of knowledge and understanding.

PEOPLE FAIL TO REALIZE HOW IMPORTANT THE WORD OF GOD IS. The word of God is the standard you will be judged by. If you don't allow the word of God to rule you, something else will. During my days of crippling anxiety, I was afraid to open my Bible and I was also afraid not to. I knew if I read it, I would be responsible for obeying what was written there.

If you are too self-absorbed you will miss what God is doing. Keep your mind on His word and listen to what it is saying. I was preoccupied with my own problems and concentrating on problems always makes them seem bigger. I was waiting on God, and He was waiting on me! I was waiting on God to help me; He was waiting on me to do what His word says!

When I finally began to read, I realized how little I knew. I simply didn't know enough to help myself! I was completely absorbed by what had happened to me, by what I had seen and learned for myself.

The Bible shows us a higher way of thinking because it contains God's own wisdom. I came to consider it a source of hidden treasures.

We are blessed to know God and to have a chance to learn His wisdom! There are so many things wisdom can teach you; have you learned to pursue it yet?

There is the question of direction. Where should you go and what should you do? Here is another question: in what direction are your thoughts headed? The Bible tells you what you should be thinking about and how to focus on the best things. Do you read it enough? Do you remember what it has to say? Do you allow its words of truth to guide your life?

I didn't spend time reading my Bible. For me, a Bible was just something we all had. We placed our Bibles prominently in our houses and carried them to church so we could follow along when the preacher quoted an occasional scripture verse.

"Where is Your Bible?"

I was talking to one woman about reading her Bible, and she said, "I don't know where my Bible is." One of her children said, "I think it fell behind the washing machine." She said, "When was that?" Her child answered: "Oh, it must have been a few months ago."

The woman hadn't even missed her Bible although it had been lost for months! Open your Bible every day and see all the good things God has for you. Health, strength, and joy are just three of His treasures!

Your Bible won't do you any good as long as it sits on the coffee table or on your desk. Open it and read it! Do you hesitate because you are afraid of what the Bible will say to you? Allow Jesus to strengthen you. Depend on Him as He leads you into a place of peace and protection. If you are struggling, you are not following God's model!

The Bible relates God's overview of history, the story of His covenants, His holy writings, prophecies, and the gospel of the Lord Jesus Christ. And remember, the Bible is a message to obey, not just to listen to. So don't fool yourselves. James 1:22 (TLB)

Go to the Bible every day to find spiritual food. I was at a prayer meeting one night and we were all praising God. After a time of praise and worship, we opened our Bibles to study. My friend said, "We have had a drink of water; now we'll eat!"

God Himself

Let me be clear. When I talk about God, Jesus, and the Holy Spirit in this book I mean God the Father Who is enthroned in heaven, Jesus Christ, Son of God and our Savior, and the Holy Spirit, third Person of the Godhead. This is the HOLY TRINITY.

God authored the Bible. His word is truth, and His salvation is real. You cannot save yourself or lead yourself. When God leads you, it will be through the voice of the HOLY SPIRIT. When you pray, you are praying to the Father in heaven. Everything you receive from Him is based on the redemptive work of the Lord Jesus Christ. See how they all work together? The Holy Spirit will never lead you contrary to God's word. Jesus is called the Word of God.

Inheritance

In Luke 15 Jesus talked about a certain man who had two sons. Neither one of his boys understood inheritance.

One of the sons asked for his share of the money and then ran off to spend it on worthless things. He is called the prodigal, or reckless, son.

The other son stayed with his father, but he only wanted to work and worry every day. He didn't understand inheritance either; he saw his father as a hard person, not a generous one.

Everything the father owned was available to both of them. They had only to rest in the knowledge of sonship!

Some Christians feel like orphans because they see God as distant, judgmental, even cold. Nothing could be further from the truth! He is always with us and will never forsake us. He has provided everything you need. Can you learn to rest in Him and trust Him?

Psalm 7:1 says, "O LORD my God, in You I put my trust."

Redemption vs. Religion

You must learn to separate REDEMPTION from RELIGION. If you are redeemed, you have been restored back to the Father's house with full inheritance. Everything He has is yours! That is redemption!

Religion demands that you keep thinking like a servant, constantly working and working yet gaining nothing. To fully understand this, go back to the story of Adam.

Adam put the dominion and privilege God gave him under Satan's control. When the earth came under Satan, it was cursed. Curses include sickness, death, mental torment, and toil.

Toil is work without reward or end. Religion and traditions of men require toil. By the time you do everything religion requires, you won't feel like worshipping God!

Religion will keep you so busy and tired that you won't have time to meditate on God's word.

Christ restored all that Adam gave away. That means you can have health, life, peace, and heirship instead of the curse. Yes, you will work but your work will be rewarded because you have dominion over your own life. Your burden will be light because Jesus has done the difficult part. Your inheritance is assured, and you won't have to toil. "The Lord's blessing is our greatest wealth. All our work adds nothing to it!" (Proverbs 10:22 TLB)

Give Your Worries to Him

I Peter 5:7 (AMP) says, "casting all your cares [all your anxieties, all your worries, and all your concerns, once and for all] on Him, for He cares about you [with deepest affection, and watches over you very carefully]."

Your worries belong on Jesus and not on you! Learn to cast all your cares on Him and release them. See Him as your burden-bearer. This will take practice and persistence! Cast your cares over and over as needed!

Deuteronomy 33:27 (AMPC) says, "The eternal God is your refuge and dwelling place, and underneath are the everlasting arms." The word "arms" indicates "the arm, the shoulder," or simply "strength." God is always there for you to lean upon.

Listen! God is closer to you than you can imagine. If you are born again, you are one spirit with him! "But he who is joined to the Lord is one spirit with Him." (I Corinthians 6:17) Let Him carry your worries. You may be in a mad rush to escape your past. But where do you go? What do you aim for?

The Hebrews 4:11 tells us that rest should be a priority. This is not talking about natural rest. His rest is what we must seek. His rest is supernatural, and it is total.

Rest

Matthew 11:28-30 says: "Come unto me, all ye that labor and are heavy laden, and I will give you rest. Take my yoke upon you and learn of me; for I am meek and lowly in heart: and ye shall find rest unto your souls. For my yoke is easy, and my burden is light."

The idea is to be yoked with Jesus and to let Him pull most of the load. Base everything you do on His victory! The victory He won will hold up under any pressure this world can bring! Link arms with Him and lean on His strength.

Psalm 6:4 (AMPC) Return [to my relief], O Lord, deliver my life; save me for the sake of Your steadfast love and mercy. God is our home! God is our Father! God is love!

Rebellion, or trusting one's own way and judgment, is called "pride." God resists the proud and gives grace to the humble. He won't help the one who stubbornly pursues his own way. Like the prodigal, we need to come back to the Father's house.

That is where restoration happens, not in the pigpen. The pigpen is where his heart and will were changed. Nothing man produces can make him holy before God because God is not impressed by outward things. He is waiting for a heart change.

- **God is love.**
- **Love never fails.**
- **God's love sent Jesus.**

Jesus triumphed over all: sin, sickness, and death. In the statement "love never fails" we see God's love and Jesus' triumph both come to a climax.

Personally Speaking

Proverbs 18:2 (ICB) reveals an important concept: "A foolish person does not want to understand anything. She only enjoys telling others what she thinks."

Have you been around someone like this? No matter what else is said, she always directs the conversation back to herself. Nothing matters except her thoughts, her opinions, and her problems.

She scorns others, even God. She doesn't need to learn His wisdom because she knows so much! Proverbs 22:10 says, "Cast out the scorner…strife and reproach shall cease."

The Hebrew word translated "scorner" in this verse means "to boast" and "to mock." It also means "to interpret."

A scorner may think she knows everything and needs no outside information. Perhaps you feel self-sufficient and able to interpret every aspect of life and scripture FOR YOURSELF!

Stop being a CRITIC and start being a STUDENT. Stop being critical of the Bible and start viewing it as a textbook. God's part is to teach, and your part is to listen, read, and learn. Focus on what God has said and believe Him no matter what feelings tell you. How important is the word of God to your recovery?

Are You Proud?

Perhaps you feel proud of yourself and even wiser than God. A person who thinks he already knows everything finds it difficult to learn.

Are you someone who always wants to be right? If so, that will work against you. You may think you have all the answers. In that case, the Bible has little to offer you.

We are told to seek God's wisdom like we were though hunting for treasure.

Proverbs 2:4 (MSG) God says we are to search for wisdom "like a prospector panning for gold, like an adventurer on a treasure hunt." Prospectors make treasure hunting their life's work. They are forever looking for that next big cache! No matter how much treasure they find they always want more!

In Proverbs 4:21 (MSG) you are told to commit God's words to memory. He says, "Keep my message in plain view at all times. Concentrate! Learn it by heart!" God has given us a wonderful way to commit something to memory: repeat it aloud. That is how you imprint something on your memory. Repeat it over and over.

Reverence for God

We have all heard that we are to fear God. What does that mean? Proverbs 8:13 (TLB) instructs, "If anyone respects and fears God, he will hate evil. For wisdom hates pride, arrogance, corruption, and deceit of every kind."

He hates sin and so should we. Why does He hate it? Sin hurts people.

Every time someone has hurt you, that person has hurt God too. Are you afraid you have committed come unforgivable sin? Nothing is unforgivable if you are trusting Jesus as your Savior.

God hates pride because it makes people rely on themselves and not on Him. He also hates self-importance. Conceited people put others down.

God also hates lying. When lies are told someone will get hurt. Evil words hurt people. Don't say them!

What does God prize? He loves gentle, quiet people and teachable spirits.

Gentle and Quiet

I Peter 3:3-4 "…the hidden person of the heart, with the incorruptible beauty of a gentle and quiet spirit, which is very precious in the sight of God."

You desire to be gentle and quiet, but can you manage it? It might seem that anger, rage, bitterness, and pain will always be part of your life. It doesn't have to be that way!

Proverbs 3:13 (AMP) states, "Happy [blessed, considered fortunate, to be admired] is the man who finds [skillful and godly] WISDOM, And the man who gains understanding and insight [learning from God's word and life's experiences]."

Don't depend on man's wisdom; listen for the still, small voice of the Holy Spirit. Natural man ignores God's word, but a person who is teachable hears it.

No amount of education, training, or brainpower can take away the importance of God's word. Nothing can decrease God's ability to save. You need Him, and you can come to Him freely!

Words You Speak

Sometimes it is better not to say anything. I asked a friend from the Middle East what was the most important advice his mother ever gave him. He remembered it well. It was: "Can you just keep your mouth shut?" The Book of Proverbs has a lot to say about this:

- Proverbs 10:19 (MSG) – "The more talk, the less truth."
- Proverbs 17:28 (TLB) – "A man of few words and settled mind is wise."
- Proverbs 29:11 (GNT) - "Stupid people express their anger openly."

Romans 13:8 says, "Owe no one anything except to love one another." Don't put yourself under obligation to people! Stay free of hastily formed plans. Make no friendship with angry or dishonest people."

It is good not to promise too much or to extend yourself too far. Sometimes people make promises in order to keep friendships, but it is God Who brings true friends into our lives. So, don't make big promises. Be loving, be generous, and be genuine. That is enough!

Guard Your Heart and Lips

Proverbs 4:23 says: "Keep your heart with all diligence, for out of it spring the issues of life."

I Peter 3:10 (TLB) says: "If you want a happy, good life, keep control of your tongue, and especially guard your lips from telling lies." Controlling the tongue is important, and references to it are all through the word of God.

Peter referenced lying. If you don't control your tongue carefully, you will speak lies about others, lies about yourself, and even lies about God! God wants you to speak truth. God cannot lie. (Titus 1:2) His word is truth. (John 17:17) God's truth will bring true peace.

Your Thought Life

Teach yourself to think lovely thoughts. It will take focus to keep out worldly thoughts such as fear, worry, and discouragement.

Philippians 4:8 says, "Finally, brethren, whatsoever things are true, whatsoever things are honest, whatsoever things are just, whatsoever things are pure, whatsoever things are lovely, whatsoever things are of good report; if there be any virtue, and if there be any praise, think on these things."

If you obey what this verse says, your thought life will be clean and productive! This will exclude all inoperative fleshly thoughts and make your mind ready to receive and remember the word of God.

Fleshly thoughts make people believe they can do things their own way without God's help. You should be especially careful to get rid of strife. Paul is explicit when discussing this.

2 Corinthians 12:20 (GW) says: "I'm afraid that I may come and find you different from what I want you to be…I'm afraid that there may be rivalry, jealousy, hot tempers, selfish ambition, slander, gossip, arrogance, and disorderly conduct."

God's Wisdom

We must receive the Word of God as final authority. We must respect and honor it more than any other source of information. We are told to make our ear attentive to it; we are told to direct our heart and mind toward it by reading the Word, memorizing it, and obeying it.

We are told to search for Wisdom in His Word as though we are seeking buried treasure. If we do all these things with a sincere heart, we will attain wisdom. Proverbs 4:20 says, "My son (or daughter) attend to My words." If you don't attend to His word and respect it, the Bible will seem to be a closed book and it won't benefit you.

He is God! "The [reverent] fear of the LORD [that is, worshiping Him and regarding Him as truly awesome] is the beginning…of knowledge." Proverbs 1:7 (AMP)

What can stop God's wisdom? Human tradition can! Jesus said, "You break the law of God in order to protect your man-made tradition." (Mark 7:13 TLB) God's word is sometimes referred to as His law.

Wisdom is set forth as a high goal, for the Bible says, "Wisdom is the principal thing." (Prov. 4:7) Everyone should seek wisdom to solve everyday problems. Understanding scripture leads to knowledge; knowledge grows until we attain wisdom. Colossians 1:9-10 says:

"For this cause we also, since the day we heard it, do not cease to pray for you, and to desire that ye might be filled with the knowledge of his will in all wisdom and spiritual understanding.

That ye might walk worthy of the Lord unto all pleasing, being fruitful in every good work, and increasing in the knowledge of God."

Understanding the ways of God is the ultimate wisdom. Then we can walk with the Lord and be fruitful in every good work.

Faith proceeds from God, so it has a beautiful elegance. It is not simple-minded as many believe! Faith works by love, and love is one of the principal signs of maturity.

Read Your Bible!

GOD'S WORD IS TRUTH, and it must become the source of your peace. Allow the Bible to guide your actions. There is a wisdom in the spiritual realm that bypasses knowledge. The Bible is a visual book and its "word pictures" speak to us.

I used to read the Bible as a religious drill. It was something I thought everyone ought to do. I wasn't trying to gain information about God.

II Peter 1:2 says, "Grace and peace be multiplied unto you through the knowledge of God, and of Jesus our Lord." Did you get that? Your peace will be multiplied through the knowledge of God, and God has revealed Himself through Jesus Christ, Who is called "the Word of God."

John 1:1 says, "In the beginning was the Word, and the Word was with God, and the Word was God." The Bible is really the story of Jesus, and Jesus is called the Word of God.

In John 8:49 Jesus says, "I honor My Father." Let's be sure to honor Him too!

Jesus reveals God to us. John 1:14 (MSG) says, "We saw the glory with our own eyes, the one-of-a-kind glory, like Father, like Son, Generous inside and out, true from start to finish."

The Bible on your bookshelf addresses every problem you will ever face, and it highlights qualities your life can possess such as love, hope, faith, and joy.

We are told how to approach God's word: "Making your ear attentive to skillful and godly Wisdom and inclining and directing your heart and mind to understanding [applying all your powers to the quest for it]." (Proverbs 2:6-9 AMPC)

Remember:

Search for God's wisdom and find it in His word! Spend time studying it!

Chapter 3: Trust

Proverbs 3:5 (GW) - Trust the LORD with all your heart, and do not rely on your own understanding.

IN ORDER TO TRUST THE LORD WITH ALL YOUR HEART you must believe that He is good. It was hard for me to accept that at first. I used to trust God a little, but not too far. I was not sure if He was really good or not.

You should trust God's Word more than you trust your own feelings. Don't just depend on what seems right to you!

The realization that you are in covenant with God must be more immediate and real to you than any fear. Don't allow feelings to slow down the workings of covenant. You possess authority over fear; use your faith, which is reliance upon covenant.

Have you been bullied, shamed, or silenced? If so, it may be hard to trust anyone. Take a step back and see who is doing these things.

Sometimes parents may seem to be too harsh, yet they are working for your benefit. Listen to the people who have authority in your life: parents, doctors, teachers, ministers. Don't take advice about important things from friends.

In God's covenant there is no one to fear and no one to impress. God's blessing is always working, and you are growing in wisdom every day as you read His word.

Faith requires patience; in other words, there is no time when you won't need faith.

Maintain your life of faith and let patience have her perfect work. Remember that patience is not merely waiting for something.

Patience is strong, prolonged faith; it is faith that is strong enough wait for the desired answer. While you are waiting, cultivate diligence and fruit of the spirit. Develop a marvelous attitude. Be thankful and cooperative! Make your time of patience a time of bearing fruit of the spirit!

God's Righteousness

God is righteous; that means He has moral excellence.

But it means more than that. It means He is so caring that He wants to draw us all up to His level. His way of doing that is covenant.

A covenant is a blood-sworn oath and is set by cutting the wrists of two participants slightly and binding them together.

Then they exchanged coats and weapons. Each one pledged to help the other in any situation or emergency. Each took on all the problems of the other. Then came a grand meal.

God entered into covenant with humanity through the blood of Jesus. He took on our sins and God gave us His righteousness. God was in Christ, reconciling us to Himself.

"Rightness"

In our culture, being "righteous" can mean being smug and conceited. The attitude of self-righteousness is repulsive to us. God's righteousness is not that way at all! It is really "rightness." God is righteous or right because of His holiness and magnificent love. He made the rules for us and wrote the Bible.

God's rightness cannot be earned. At the time of new birth each child of God is declared righteous by Jesus Christ Who holds the scepter of righteousness.

Hebrews 1:8 says, "But unto the Son he saith, Thy throne, O God, is for ever and ever: a sceptre of righteousness is the sceptre of thy kingdom." Psalms 45:6 says, "Thy throne, O God, is for ever and ever: the sceptre of thy kingdom is a right sceptre." A scepter is a jeweled staff, a symbol of kingship.

We see that Psalm 45 uses the word "right" and Hebrews records that as "righteousness." Jesus used His scepter of righteousness to cause us to be born again when He gave His own rightness to us. When He lays His scepter of rightness on a heart, He makes it like His heart. Doubt and unbelief are removed.

The founder of a group or club makes rules for it and declares what is "right" for members. Remember that God established a family, and He made His children in His image. He wants them to act like Him; He declares them righteous like Him.

When you were born, you were given a name. That name identified you as part of a family. It still does! Who is included in family gatherings, strangers or family members? Family gatherings are for family members!

If a child disobeys, runs away from home, or ruins his new clothes, he is still a member of the family. His status hasn't changed at all! You are righteous if you have acknowledged Jesus as your Savior and Lord.

God's kingdom is for the righteous, and rightness is conferred when they are born again. Jesus Christ uses a "scepter of righteousness" to make each one right. That is why He assured Nicodemus "you must be born again."

So, righteousness can never be earned. It is the birthright of every born-again child of God. Rightness is right-standing with God, and it is a permanent condition. Nothing can increase it or decrease it.

God Demands Faith

Hebrews 11:6 (TLB) says: "You can never please God without faith, without depending on Him.

Anyone who wants to come to God must believe that there is a God and that He rewards those who sincerely look for Him."

God's written word turns us to His way of thinking. As we learn His words and ways, we understand Him more and more.

He wants us to have faith. The Bible tells us four times: "the just shall live by faith." How can you do that? You can pray and expect answers.

If you are born again, you are righteous, and His ears are open to your prayers. 1 John 5:15 says, "And if we know that he hears us, whatsoever we ask, we know that we have the petitions that we desired of him."

Jesus: Author and Finisher of our Faith

Have confidence in God's word. Have faith in God, in Jesus Christ your REDEEMER, and in His word. Your faith depends on Jesus, Author and Finisher of our faith. (Hebrews 12:2)

Jesus tells us to have faith in God or to have "the God kind of faith."

The God kind of faith calls things into being that do not yet exist. This is how the world was created. As His children, we have dominion over our own lives.

There is no "blind faith" where covenant is concerned. We know exactly what we are going to get and exactly what our faith can produce. The New Testament presents guidelines for covenant living: forgiveness for sin, healing for mind and body, provision for this life, and a secure and blessed eternity.

In addition, we have access to God and are able to enjoy His fellowship, protection, instruction, victory, and joy. Faith comes as we read and hear the word of God. (Romans 10:17)

Covenant Promises

Covenant swearing in the Old Testament depended on each partner knowing beforehand exactly what he was sworn to receive. Learn to trust and rest. If you are worrying, you are not resting. Worry interferes with faith and slows down your answer.

If you are going to rest in Him, you will have to refuse worry and care. Covenant partners must trust each other and know for sure that the other partner will perform his job and fulfill his promises. Trust encourages learning and exploration. As you explore the Bible you will have questions. Ask God to give you answers.

- **Read His word.**
- **Form questions and record them.**
- **Look for answers in His word.**
- **Ask God for revelation.**

Answers may come in unexpected ways, but God is always gentle and good. Be aware that He never teaches through sickness, disease, or hardship.

God never wants you to be sick! Jeremiah 32:41 says, "God rejoices over us to do us good."

We are told to find wisdom in His word. We are also told that the Holy Spirit Himself will teach those who are born again.

Authority

Within the word "authority" is "author." An author is one who has authority to write, either by personal experience or by careful research. Who has the authority to assure us that we are forgiven when we confess to God?

Jesus does! He died for our sins and was raised for our justification. He presented Himself before the Father in heaven. His New Covenant will stand forever.

Jesus has become a SURETY, or guarantee, of a better covenant. (Heb. 7:22) We believe His word. We become more and more Christlike as we are transformed into His likeness.

Confidence

If you ask God for something, and you know He has heard you, you can be confident He will answer your prayer. When you have confidence, you can keep words of faith in your mouth. Speak like God will answer because He will!

In Job, there was no daysman or intercessor found. Solomon said, "There is no one to comfort [me]." (emphasis is mine) Christ fulfills all of these needs.

He became our Intercessor, the only One Who can bring us to God. He is our wisdom. He is the Redeemer Whose blood was precious enough to pay the price for us. He sent the Holy Spirit to be our Comforter and Teacher.

No Formulas Please!

You shouldn't try to make God's precious word into a set of formulas! You can believe God, confess His word, declare what you want to happen, and receive God's answers by faith. This is what the Bible instructs us to do.

Pray to the Father in Jesus' name. Don't place your faith in prayer itself. Don't place faith in any mere person or in someone else's prayers. Focus your faith directly on Jesus Christ your Champion.

Philippians 4:6 says: Be careful for nothing; but in everything by prayer and supplication with thanksgiving let your requests be made known unto God. To be careful for nothing means "Don't worry." Be sure to thank God for the answer when it comes!

Faith: Our Confidence in Him

We must have faith in God to get saved, and He gives us a measure of faith. We learn to depend on God more and more, and our faith, our confidence in Him, grows. What is faith? Faith is steadfast confidence in God and in His word; it is absolute commitment to Jesus as your Redeemer. What difference does faith in God and in His word make?

"Now this is the confidence that we have in Him, that if we ask anything according to His will, He hears us. And if we know that He hears us, whatever we ask, we know that we have the petitions that we have asked of Him." (I John 5:14-15)

Faith gives us certainty that God has heard our prayers and that He has granted our petitions. This seems presumptuous to many, but the secret of answered prayer is to ask only for things He has already given to believers.

God has already granted "all things pertaining to life and godliness." II Peter 1:3 says,

"According as his divine power hath given unto us all things that pertain unto life and godliness, through the knowledge of him that hath called us to glory and virtue."

Notice that this comes through "the knowledge of Him that has called us to glory and virtue." Knowledge of Jesus' redemption comes, then commitment to Him must follow if you are to be saved. By means of faith, He places believers in a position of authority over their own lives.

Jesus commanded mountains, trees, wind, waves, and sickness. We look to Jesus, Author and Finisher of our faith (Hebrews 12:2).

Finisher mean "developer." He develops our faith so we can stay steadfastly focused on His great victory over sin, sickness, and death!

Don't just have a generic, random kind of faith; Jesus said, "Have faith in God." Some translations say, "Have the faith of God."

Truth

God fashioned the New Covenant. He will keep His part. Some people think God is not dependable, that He is ever-changing.
Malachi 3:6 declares that God NEVER CHANGES. He is never impulsive. Since so much depends on truth, shouldn't we commit ourselves to being truthful?

- We worship God in spirit and truth. John 4:23
- Jesus said He is the Truth. John 14:6
- Jesus said God's word is Truth. John 17:17
- The Holy Spirit is the Spirit of Truth. John 14:7
- The Truth sanctifies. John 17:9

Watch Your Words

The greatest problems in the body of Christ stem from words.

Christians say things they shouldn't say! They gossip. They speak words of doubt and unbelief.

Much has been written and preached to wake the church up to this fact. You must pay attention to the things you say! How can we do this? James 3:2-4 tells us: "For we all stumble in many things. If anyone does not stumble in word, he is a perfect man, able also to bridle the whole body.

Indeed, we put bits in horses' mouths that they may obey us, and we turn their whole body.

Look also at ships: although they are so large and are driven by fierce winds, they are turned by a very small rudder wherever the pilot desires." (NKJV)

The word "perfect" in verse 2 may be translated "mature." Don't let the idea of spiritual growth intimidate you. The Holy Spirit knew how to get you born again and He knows how to make you grow.

He can bring you out of a spiritually dark place and cause you to hear what you need to hear. Listen to His sweet voice! What will take place at the same time? The enemy will come and try to steal the word from your heart. He will accuse you to yourself, telling you that you are really weak, afraid, and defeated.

Overcome the enemy with the word of God! If you have memorized verses from your Bible, the devil will not be able to steal them. If you know who you are in Christ-an overcomer-the devil will not be able to deceive you into thinking you are defeated.

Your Covenant Partner

Your covenant Partner will lead you and defend you. He is your rear guard. He leads you into the future and protects you from past mistakes. Isaiah 58:8 explains this. "Then your light will break out like the dawn, And your healing (restoration, new life) will quickly spring forth; Your righteousness will go before you [leading you to peace and prosperity], The glory of the LORD will be your rear guard." In other words, do your best and trust Him to take care of the rest!

Look to Jesus

Jesus not only invented our faith, He completed our faith. We will always have all the faith we need as we focus on His word and on Him.

Hebrews 12:2 says, "Looking unto Jesus the author and finisher of our faith; who for the joy that was set before him endured the cross, despising the shame, and is set down at the right hand of the throne of God."

Jesus is Author of faith and its Finisher. An author invents and a finisher completes. The author of a book has something in common with an artist. What would their work be without finishing touches?

Look at the last part of that verse. "...for the joy that was set before him endured the cross, despising the shame, and is set down at the right hand of the throne of God."

He has seated Himself on God's throne. All the work necessary for you to have faith has been done! As He said, "It is finished!" Now, read the word and grow in maturity!

Defeat is a mindset!

Hear what the word of God says! "For a righteous man may fall seven times And rise again." The word "seven" carries the idea of completeness.

So, a righteous person may face a devastating defeat it seems impossible to recover from. However, that same believer can rise victorious.

Problems are always temporary. Do not allow the fact that you fell into difficulty become a mindset of depression and failure. Pain and problems will not teach you anything! However, in the midst of trouble, God can show you how to overcome.

You Are Righteous!

You are the righteousness of God in Christ. Anything that challenges Christ's victory in your life must be eliminated from your thinking. What does the Bible say about you? You have life, peace, victory, love, and authority. Any thoughts that disagree must fall away.

- Defeat falls before Christ's victory.
- Hatred falls before Christ's love.
- Confusion gives way to Christ's peace.
- His strength conquers weakness.
- His life triumphs over death.

Are you accustomed to suffering? Do you expect it? Break that mindset! Faith does not expect suffering; it expects answers to prayer!

Don't allow your mind, will, and emotions to be taken captive by toxic thoughts. Put those thoughts off! Concentrate on the fact that you are righteous!

"I will greatly rejoice in the LORD, my soul shall be joyful in my God; for he hath clothed me with the garments of salvation, he hath covered me with the robe of righteousness…" (Isaiah 61:10)

It is important to plan for the future. Go ahead and set some goals and list things you want to accomplish. You will not accomplish all your goals, because no one does, but you can reach some of them. You can fulfil God's plan for your life!

God will direct this process too, and you should TRUST Him to do it! Proverbs 16:9 (TLB) "We should make plans—counting on God to direct us." All of this is part of faith.

Remember:

"TRUST IN AND RELY CONFIDENTLY ON THE LORD with all your heart And do not rely on your own insight or understanding." Proverbs 3:5 (AMP)

Learn to have faith in the Lord and rely on Him with your whole heart.

Chapter 4: Healing

Proverbs 3:8 (TLB) - You will be given renewed health and vitality.

I WANTED TO BE HEALTHY AND FREE, but I was depending only on natural ways to accomplish that. I tried to rest as much as possible so I could get well, but resting was impossible because I was worrying night and day.

See, my body could not heal because my thoughts were toxic. On the other hand, my toxic thoughts caused continual bodily weakness and exhaustion. I was trapped in a vicious cycle. What was happening to me? My life was severely limited, and I even became housebound.

In this fallen world, things change, and they deteriorate. I had to overcome physical problems and get done what must be done, like finding a job. Things needed to be maintained and that would require more work.

Mark 16:18 describes God's will for the sick: "They shall recover." The word "recover" means "to be well, to be in a good place, to be comfortable." How could I reach that place of recovery and health?

"Inner Healing"

Many ministers teach about "inner healing" and attempt to mix some sort of counselling with faith in God's word and the laying on of hands. Beware of this! You don't have to reveal your inmost thoughts and be "counselled" in order to receive healing from God. Church services and prayer lines are not the proper place for counselling!

It is not necessary to tell your deepest secrets to another human being in order to be healed, but if you do need professional counselling, the Holy Spirit will help you find the right doctor, counsellor, or clinic. Seek His leading!

If you feel overwhelmed by problems, actively search for solutions. Ask for help! Learn ways to relieve the pressure. Don't just sink into hopelessness.

Things will go wrong in this broken world. You have made mistakes and so have others, but there are always actions you can take to help yourself.

When I was not yet eighteen, decisions that set the course for my life were made by my parents. My father chose to drink and gamble away his salary each week and to be abusive; my mother chose to remain silent and passively accept the consequences of his actions.

Many years later, I sought out a licensed family counsellor. That provided a chance for me to tell my troubles to a sympathetic person and brainstorm for answers. The church-based counsellor was not just a well-intentioned church member; he was a Christian professional!

He used the Bible to help me break out of a cycle of depression and hopelessness, firmly convinced that there was always hope in God. After listening sympathetically, he used what might be called "godly common sense" to gently direct my thoughts away from my painful past and towards the future!

There was always fresh coffee in his office but what he really offered was "a cup of cold water."

One day he asked, "Let's say God has made a way for you to fulfil your dreams. What would you like to do?"

College had seemed out of reach before; now, it seemed possible. My answer was, "I want to go to college." He smiled. "Another lady I counselled has just graduated with her degree in teaching. Would you like to be a teacher?"

Would I? That sounded like heaven to me! The thought of trading depression for books, papers, and study seemed too wonderful to be true!

"Yes!"

"Then this will be our final counselling session. You have chosen a worthy goal, and I am sure you will achieve it."

Before long, I was taking my first college course. Because I had lived in the household of an alcoholic father for several years, I also attended Al Anon meetings. Al Anon is a support group for family members of alcoholics. Learning that others had overcome similar problems made them seem less devastating.

Recovery is a process, and you will need to pray for leading and then do what God leads you to do. We all face an evil world, but He can show you how to overcome evil with good!

Trends

I have just mentioned one trend that made its way through the church in times past: "inner healing" sessions which depended on counselling with untrained workers. Other trends have breezed through the church also.

One of these trends was "public confession," and it included having believers reveal their most intimate thoughts, feelings, and problems in front of a group of people publicly during a prayer meeting or worship service.

Don't be persuaded to do this. It is neither necessary nor wise. Don't discuss your problems with friends or relatives either. It may be tempting to pour out your heart to someone but hold back. Going over and over problems will not help you solve them!

Another dangerous fad teaches "we've all got problems," and therefore we should just live with our troubles and not ask for God's help." This is not biblical! God wants you to recover and be completely whole. Don't give up. Don't stop praying!

There are plenty of so-called "life coaches" available too. They may offer help but many of them have been heavily influenced by New Age thinking. Don't hire them!

Barriers to Healing

Recognize barriers to your own healing within your own heart such as unforgiveness, or bitterness. Sometimes bitterness can seem like a protection against the world around you. Refuse to be bitter. Let God be your protection!

Lack of wisdom will hinder you. If you don't have knowledge of how the Bible instructs us to live, you will continue to make the same mistakes over and over.

But there were also physical factors contributing to my problem. I had lived in panic mode during high school because of my father's alcoholism.

We often lacked essentials such as transportation, electricity, water, and food. Poor nutrition, constant exposure to the elements, inability to rest, and "adrenalin blowout" had caused many physical problems.

"Incurable"

Get rid of the idea that your problems are incurable. My mother and grandmother were convinced that some women are destined to live nervous, fearful, sickly lives. They even told me I was one of those unfortunate women!

They named my weaknesses "incurable," and insisted there was little hope of recovery. It all became so very mysterious!

The Amplified Bible says Jesus took our pain, sickness, weakness, and distress. (Isaiah 53:4 AMPC) This does not refer only to physical problems. He also heals mental distress brought about by the curse. Jesus took it all upon Himself!

Jeremiah 30:17 (MSG) says, "I will cure the incurable."

Deuteronomy 28:59 (AMP) says, “severe and lasting plagues, and miserable and chronic sicknesses” are under the curse of the law. The Message says, “every disease and catastrophe imaginable” is under the curse.
Illnesses lasting a long time are under the curse, and you are redeemed from them! Jesus is the Mediator of a better covenant, which was established on better promises. (Hebrews 8:6)
Galatians 3:13 (NKJV) says, “Christ has redeemed us from the curse of the law, having become a curse for us (for it is written, “Cursed is everyone who hangs on a tree”). Did Christ hang on a tree? Yes! Was He cursed? Yes! He was cursed with the curse of the law so those who believe on Him could be redeemed. (If you are taking prescription medicines, do not stop taking them unless that action is approved by your doctor!)

Diseases lasting of long duration can be healed:

- Blind Bartimaeus
- Crippled man at Gate Beautiful

  Woman with the issue of blood

God Gives Healing and Health.

The centurion asked Jesus to "speak the word only" when his servant needed to be healed. Jesus called the centurion's faith "great." You may not be able to go to church or have a minister pray for you. The Lord has already spoken healing over you.

Healing Rests on Jesus' Finished Work.

Isaiah 53:5 (AMPC) says, "But He was wounded for our transgressions, He was bruised for our guilt and iniquities; the chastisement [needful to obtain] peace and well-being for us was upon Him, and with the stripes [that wounded] Him we are healed and made whole.

This is the Lord's declaration of healing for you; "with the stripes [that wounded] Him we are healed and made whole."

What is Your Part?

God made Adam to have dominion.

Genesis 1:26-28 (NKJV) says: 26 Then God said, "Let Us make man in Our image, according to Our likeness; let them have dominion… 27 So God created man in His own image; in the image of God He created him; male and female He created them. 28 Then God blessed them, and God said to them, "Be fruitful and multiply; fill the earth and subdue it; have dominion… [Some words have been omitted by the author for emphasis.]

We see that man has the ability to speak, and man has been given dominion over animals and birds who can't. So, the WORDS of man express man's dominion. Knowing this, we must watch our words!

As you take time to learn what the Bible says you will learn how to control your own thoughts and words. This is how you take dominion over your own life!

Jesus Paid Our Debt

The common Hebrew word for "double" means "to fold over," or "double as a cloth"), and this word means a double portion.

That is simple, but Isaiah 40:2 uses a different word. It uses a Hebrew term which carries a special meaning.

"Speak ye comfortably to Jerusalem, and cry unto her, that her warfare is accomplished, that her iniquity is pardoned: for she hath received of the Lord's hand DOUBLE for all her sins." (Isaiah 40:2)

This word is literally "The double." It is the Hebrew word "Kif-la-yim" from the root word "kaphal," and it is an idiom.

It is Strong's 3718, "The double," with a Hebrew article "THE," and it occurs only three times in the Old Testament: Job 41:13, Job 11:16, Isaiah 40:2.

To give someone "the double" in Old Testament times meant to take the little scroll their debts were written on and double it over. It amounted to a public declaration, and it meant "I will pay all your debts." This is what Jesus did about our sins; He paid for them!

You can receive "THE DOUBLE" from God today because Jesus has already taken your judgment and punishment. He is always ready and willing to forgive!

When someone would give THE DOUBLE" to a debtor, he lifted the head of that person.

You see, a debtor was obliged to walk around looking down. Lifting of the head was another sign of freedom from debt. Psalm 3:3 says: "But thou, O LORD, art a shield for me; my glory, and the lifter up of mine head." See, the pain people experience is all the result of sin. Jesus is your great Redeemer Who has taken your debt of sin and shame! You can be free of it, and you can forgive others! He has paid your debt and lifted your head. Rejoice!

Prince of Peace

Jesus is the Prince of Peace. He brings peace with God. The Hebrew word is "shalom," which means "nothing missing, and nothing broken." You can have recovery now because He was broken for you.

You may think, "That's just too simple. You can't imagine what I have been through." No, I don't know, but God does!

He knows all of the heartache and heartbreak, and the whole story of abuse, mistreatment, neglect, and pain. You may not be able to trust my words, but you can trust His!

Religion teaches that God wants to break us. No, He wants to heal us. Then, He wants us to desire His ways. First, choose His words, then choose His ways. He has already forgiven our debts and delivered us from evil.

Isaiah 9:6 says, "His name shall be called Wonderful, Counsellor, The mighty God, The everlasting Father, The Prince of Peace."

The New Testament reveals that Jesus Christ has redeemed us and has paid for our sins. His blood does not merely cover, it TRANSFORMS. If you are in Christ, you are a new creature! The Prince of Peace can now govern your life.

We have received the very life of God Himself! He has welcomed us into His family with full privileges! Jesus will always hear and answer you. His word is rich with comfort if you know where to look.

He Will Strengthen You

Some negative thought patterns are ingrained when we are children. You will not be able, in one lifetime, and in a fallen world, to overcome all these negatives perfectly.

That is why love and forgiveness are so important! You may feel weak and inadequate. You may feel like people are bombarding you with cannon balls and you have nothing to throw back except marshmallows! Are you oversensitive? You can change! Grow toward a different mindset.

Some people are introverts, and some are introverts. Introverts can become more outgoing, and extroverts can become more reserved. In the same way, you can choose God's ways over mere human behavior.

If you are too sensitive to things around you, let God harden you to difficulties. Isaiah 41:10 says, "Fear not [there is nothing to fear], for I am with you; do not look around you in terror and be dismayed, for I am your God.

I will strengthen and harden you to difficulties, yes, I will help you; yes, I will hold you up and retain you with My [victorious] right hand of rightness and justice."

If you are too self-absorbed, you will miss what God is doing in the spiritual realm. Keep your mind centered on Him, listen to Him, and do what He says!

Exalt His Name

Psalm 34:3 - O magnify the LORD with me and let us exalt his name together.

To magnify the Lord is to honor and respect Him, to focus on Him and bring Him into the center of your thoughts. Begin to see Him as the foundation of your life. He is the One you need to respect. He is the One you need to please! Honor Him and praise His name!

Millions of people are not sure whether God is listening to their prayers or not. There is one way to be certain! If you are one of His covenant ones, His ears are open to your prayers.

When you know He hears, you know deliverance is on the way. If you are hurting, He is close to you.

He will take an active part in helping you recover from heartache, tragedy, and loss.

Look directly to Jesus, Author and Finisher of your healing. Allow Him to lead and encourage you throughout the healing process! WHEN EVERYTHING ELSE FALLS AWAY, THE WORD OF GOD WILL STAY. The world around you may change, but the word of God is everlasting.

Remember:

Proverbs 3:8 TLB says, "You will be given renewed health and vitality."

Receive God's healing and health through the redemptive work of Jesus Christ.

Chapter 5: Correction

Proverbs 3:11 (TLB) - Do not resent it when God chastens and corrects you.

I REALLY DIDN'T WANT GOD TO CORRECT ME; deep inside, I was afraid of Him. I didn't realize that God wanted to adjust my focus lovingly so I could see exactly how I should live every day.

Religion tends to push people down and keep them feeling guilty. God's word lifts you up and keeps you in peace. Even His correction brings peace and stability because your repentance enables Him to remove faults and shame you carry deep inside.

God corrects because He loves. Revelation 3:19 (NLT) says, "I correct and discipline everyone I love. So be diligent and turn from your indifference." And He corrects as a Father.

Hebrews 12:7 (GW) says, "God corrects you as a father corrects his children. All children are disciplined by their fathers."

God corrects by speaking to your spirit and telling you specifically what you have done wrong. His voice will be heard within your conscience. God's correction may make you uncomfortable temporarily, but it will make your life so much better in the long run!

When you follow the world's way, your life will produce bad results (Galatians 5:19-21)

Don't Live a Dangerous Lifestyle

1. Anger – Make no friendship with an angry man; and with a furious man thou shalt not go. (Proverbs 22:24)

2. Depression - Why art thou cast down, O my soul? Hope thou in God… (Psalm 42:5)

3. Fear and Anxiousness – There is no fear in love; but perfect love casts out fear because fear involves torment. But he who fears has not been made perfect in love. (I John 4:18)

4. Unforgiveness – As you stand praying, forgive. (Mark 11:25)

5. Pride - For all that is in the world, the lust of the flesh, and the lust of the eyes, and the pride of life, is not of the Father, but is of the world. (I John 2:16)

Don't Use Wrong Words.

Once words have been spoken, processes are set in motion that will eventually bring forth bad fruit. Idle words will have to be accounted for. "But I say unto you, that every idle word men shall speak, they shall give account thereof in the day of judgment." Matthew 12:36.

I Peter 3:10 says, For he that will love life, and see good days, let him refrain his tongue from evil, and his lips that they speak no guile [sly, devious speech].

Lying A truthful witness never lies; a false witness always lies. (Proverbs 14:5 TLB)

Cursing	"You must not use the name of the Lord your God thoughtlessly. The Lord will punish anyone who is guilty and misuses his name. (Exodus 20:7 ICB)
Gossip	So then, get rid of all evil and all lying. Do not be 9 Do not be jealous or speak evil of others. (I Peter 2:1 ICB)
Complaining	These are grumblers, complainers, walking according to their own lusts; and they mouth great swelling words. (Jude 16 NKJV)
Bitterness	Do not be bitter or angry or mad. Never shout angrily or say things to hurt others. Never do anything evil. Eph. 4:31 (ICB)

Watch out for faults that are not so obvious, too. Stop using the language of hopelessness. Don't constantly repeat that you are desperate, lonely, and depressed.

Stop trying to get sympathy for people. Even if they do sympathize, the feeling of justification you'll get won't last.

The word "patient" has sometimes been used to describe a condition that might be called spiritual paralysis. I was often told by others, "Just be patient a little while longer." They meant I was supposed to sit by with resignation and wait, but God's kind of patience is active.

Having godly patience actually means stretching your faith out over an extended period of time. Hebrews 6:12 says, "That ye be not slothful, but followers of them who through faith and patience inherit the promises."

Luke 8:15 (AMP) says, "But as for that [seed] in the good soil, these are [the people] who, hearing the Word, hold it fast in a just (noble, virtuous) and worthy heart, and steadily bring forth fruit with patience." It takes fruit a while to grow and the growers must remain patient until it is ripe.

Romans 5:4 (TLB) says, "And patience develops strength of character in us and helps us trust God more each time we use it until finally our hope and faith are strong and steady." We might say that faith stretched out over a long period of time becomes stronger.

Truly the signs of an apostle were wrought among you in all patience, in signs, and wonders, and mighty deeds. (II Corinthians 12:12) So, the patient person brings forth fruit, grows in faith and hope, and even does mighty deeds.

James 1:4 sums it up: "But let patience have her perfect work, that ye may be perfect and entire, wanting nothing." Patience is active!

Don't Have Grudges

Don't have grudges or hardness in your heart against anyone. Is there a person you can't stand? You need to forgive! Forgiving others is a sure way to make your own life better. You can smooth out your own path by letting go of all grudges. Forgive everyone! Jesus said the Heavenly Father won't forgive us if we don't forgive.

If you refuse to forgive, you are not serious about getting well. If someone doesn't treat you right just forgive and forget!

Hebrews 12:15 (TLB) warns us not to become bitter. "Watch out that no bitterness takes root among you, for as it springs up it causes deep trouble, hurting many."

Who Are Your Friends?

I Corinthians 15:33 warns, "Bad company ruins good manners." Don't hang out with people who live harmful lifestyles and speak wrong words. Why? If you do, you will learn to talk and act like them!

If your friends gossip and hold grudges, you will be tempted to do the same. If your friends fail to respect their parents, you will be tempted to disrespect yours. Why live like that? Why put yourself at risk? Choose godly friends!

Psalm 1:1 - Oh, the joys of those who do not follow evil men's advice, who do not hang around with sinners, scoffing at the things of God.

The Holy Spirit will lead you, but you must listen to Him. If you feel uncomfortable around a particular person, if you detect that something just isn't right, that may be leading from the Holy Spirit. Avoid that individual!

Children are often taught to love everyone. Loving people doesn't mean opening yourself up to their problems, conversation, and habits. Let the Holy Spirit show you how to spend your time and who you should spend it with.

Sadness

For some, mourning and sadness have become a way of life. They want to be known as people who are suffering on and on. Put off sadness and make Jesus Christ your King. Look to the future and expect victory in every area of your life!

Isaiah 61:3 shows forth God's plan: "To appoint unto them that mourn in Zion, to give unto them beauty for ashes, the oil of joy for mourning, the garment of praise for the spirit of heaviness."

Imagine that a lovely rose has been burned to ashes. All its softness, delicate color, and fragrance are gone. In Bible, ashes are a symbol of sorrow and mourning. Perhaps you feel like your soul has been utterly destroyed.

You don't have to live in sorrow, regret, and hopelessness. God can restore you! He is gentle enough and caring enough to accomplish it! Look at this prophecy about the coming of Jesus.

Isaiah 61:3 (MSG) says, "GOD sent me to announce the year of his grace— a celebration of God's destruction of our enemies— and to comfort all who mourn, To care for the needs of all who mourn in Zion, give them bouquets of roses instead of ashes."

Self-Confidence

If you depend on self-confidence instead of God, you are surely headed for failure. You are not strong enough or smart enough to solve all your own problems. If you fail in some way, the incident will result in more fear!

Confidence is good, but only if it is based on God and His word. Proverbs 1:32 (AMPC) says, "For the backsliding of the simple shall slay them, and the careless ease of [self-confident] fools shall destroy them." (Emphasis is from the translation.)

Why does this verse mention "ease"? Over-the-top self-confidence leads people to become lazy and even proud. But it is impossible to walk in pride while you are leaning on God.

Your own dangerous lifestyle affects YOU the most. Anger and fear, turned upon yourself for past MISTAKES, keeps your focus on those mistakes so keenly! Regret turns into SHAME. Anger turns into rage. Fear turns into panic.

Anger, Fear, Shame, and Blame

Perhaps you blame yourself for something that has happened. Because we all have regrets, many think depression can scarcely be avoided.

Rage strikes out; panic blindly runs and hides. Anger, fear, shame, and blame about past mistakes and past hurts can overwhelm and exhaust you until you become more and more defensive and withdrawn. If this cycle is firmly established, depression can begin to control your life.

Perhaps you live distressing scenes over and over in your thoughts. Each flashback compounds your fear and anger.

Only one thing is needed to lock you into prolonged depression: PRIDE. This is the belief that fear is inevitable or that you can break the cycle of anxiety yourself, without anyone's help.

Being over-emotional can cause decisions be irrational. You are desperate to escape fear and failure. This type of chronic or prolonged depression may require medication, but that will not CURE the problems.

How can you cure your mind, your thoughts, your emotions, your SOUL? The Psalmist talked to his soul!

"O my soul, why be so gloomy and discouraged? Trust in God! I shall again praise him for his wondrous help; he will make me smile again, for he is my God!" (Psalm 42:5 TLB)

If you want a spiritual answer, first believe that God doesn't want your life to be frozen by shame or blame. We know this because Jesus actually carried your shame along with your sins and sicknesses. If you trust in Him, you can be rid of shame and even the memory of past mistakes.

Isaiah 54:4 (NKJV) - "Do not fear, for you will not be ashamed; Neither be disgraced, for you will not be put to shame; For you will forget the shame of your youth,

Psalm 25:2 (NKJV) - O my God, I trust in You; Let me not be ashamed; Let not my enemies triumph over me.

Romans 9:33 says, As it is written: "Behold, I lay in Zion a stumbling stone and rock of offense, And whoever believes on Him will not be put to shame."

When you are born again you become like a new baby who has no past. You can start over! If you believe all your shame and blame has fallen upon Jesus, you will be free. Don't assume this answer is too simplistic!

Every "word picture" in the Bible illustrates a truth. Jesus said in prayer to God, "Your word is truth." (John 17:17) What is the truth about your life?

- Jesus carried your sin. - He was wounded and bruised for our sins.
- Jesus carried your sickness. He was lashed—and we were healed!
- Jesus carried your shame. - He was despised, and we didn't care.
- Jesus carried your guilt. – He was beaten that we might have peace. (Isaiah 53:3-5 TLB)

What is the result? "Who will accuse those whom God has chosen? God has approved of them." (Romans 8:33 GW) You can be free from guilt and shame!

Rejection

Give honor where honor is due but avoid the scoffers and scorners if you can. It is not always possible to stay clear of a bitter boss, but you can choose not to drink coffee with an obnoxious neighbor!

How do you come to feel accepted? You can achieve a great goal like completing college or securing a job you want and exceling at it. Don't faint or get discouraged!

Know that you do have worth. Be steadfast and immoveable! Remember than God created man to take dominion. Unsaved people try to do that without God's guidance and blessing because they just want to make others buckle under pressure. If you have an ungodly boss, carry out instructions without bowing to pressure to talk back.

What should change you? God's word should be able to change your actions and your goals. Also, if things seem to be falling apart, pray for direction. Diligence is good, but diligence turns into zeal without knowledge if you are headed in the wrong direction.

Many people have certitude within themselves, but we should have certainty in the word of God. The word contains our guiding principles. Fearing rejection can bring you into association with the wrong people. Many Christians are lonely because they never get to know God. And loneliness can paralyze!

"May the Lord lift up His countenance upon you" means "may the Lord smile at you." He smiles because He loves you. He smiles because you are accepted in the beloved. He smiles when you do what He asks you to do!

Now, who is competent to judge you? Your pastor? Your family? Your friends? No. Only God is! He sees your heart.

The Golden Chain

II Peter 1:5-8 (NKJV) is sometimes called the "golden chain." It lists several qualities a Christian believer should have.

5. But also for this very reason, giving all diligence, add to your faith virtue, to virtue knowledge,
6. to knowledge self-control, to self-control perseverance, to perseverance godliness,
7. to godliness brotherly kindness, and to brotherly kindness love.
8. For if these things are yours and abound, you will be neither [e]barren nor unfruitful in the knowledge of our Lord Jesus Christ.

Peter has given us the recipe for a successful Christian life. When we are born again each of us receives a measure of faith.

- To faith add virtue, or excellence.
- To excellence add knowledge.
- To knowledge add temperance, or self-control.
- To temperance add patience.
- To patience add godliness.
- To godliness add brotherly kindness.
- To brotherly kindness add charity.

In the Roman world, the term "virtue" carried the idea of moral excellence and strength. When you are born again, God gives you a measure of faith. (a measure of flour in Bible days was a little over a bushel.)

Keep adding to your faith by hearing and reading the Bible. To faith add high moral standards. You will need them in order to stand strong, to be steadfast!

Then, you will need temperance, or self-control. Stop every impulse that does not conform to the character of Christ.

To temperance add patience. Learn to stretch your self-control out over a long period of time. Then you will have the power to wait and choose how to act, and not be carried or bullied into reckless actions and words.

To patience add godliness; choose to do only good. Be persistent and steadfast in voicing your prayers of faith and in actively watching for them to be answered!
To godliness add brotherly kindness. Learn how to truly love one another. To brotherly kindness add charity or covenant love and loyalty.

Be Pleasing to Him!

Colossians 1:10 (ICB) says, "Then you will live the kind of life that honors and pleases the Lord in every way. You will produce fruit in every good work and grow in the knowledge of God."

There are some qualities you should have:

- humility – let others go first
- meekness – be willing to learn, teachable
- patience – have self-control, even under pressure
- love – accept others in the love of Christ
- peace - be one in the Spirit, and be at peace with each other.

It is time for you to read the New Testament with fresh eyes. You will have to forgive others and keep peace with them no matter how they treat you! In order to do this, draw upon the things God has provided for your life.

- We have the Peace of Christ.
  [John 14:27, John 16:33, Rom. 10:15, 14:7]

- We have the patience of Christ.
  [Luke 8:15, Col. 1:11, I Tim. 6:11, James 1:3]

- We have the purpose of Christ.
  [Phil, 3:14, Eph. 1:12 (TLB), Phil. 1:27 (TLB)]

- We have the power of Christ.
  [I Cor. 4:20, Mat. 10:1, Luke 24:49, Acts 1:8]

- We have the perfection of Christ.
  [Mat. 5:8, Luke 6:40, John 17:23, II Cor. 13:11].

Fruit of the Spirit

But when the Holy Spirit controls our lives, we will produce those good qualities, the fruit of the spirit found in Galatians 5:22-23:

love
joy
peace
patience
kindness
goodness
faithfulness
gentleness
self-control

The New Testament admonishes us to seek perfection, or maturity, in Christ. By faith, we can have it. If your faith is lacking, use His!

You might ask, "Who am I to believe His promises will be fulfilled in my life?" You are His child! This is how you rely on your Heavenly Father!

Paul connects PERFECTION to PURPOSE in Philippians 3:12 – "Not as though I had already attained, either were already perfect: but I follow after, if that I may apprehend that for which also I am apprehended of Christ Jesus."

Searching

Searching and dissatisfaction are not always wrong. Sometimes a holy restlessness invades your heart so you will raise your eyes and look for God's answers. God will raise your sights to the prospect of something better. If you are aiming too low, He will help you fix your gaze on a higher goal. This does not mean living in some sort of fantasy land.

You need to be aware of two realms. One of them is the spiritual realm, the realm of faith, light, love, God's word, and fruit of the spirit. The other is the fallen world that lives under Satan's dominion. That fallen world includes sickness, weakness, and disease.

The Holy Spirit will direct you how to walk in the spirit and how to pray. Don't pray from a place of desperation. Walk in the light!

What has God already promised? DO NOT RESENT IT WHEN GOD CHASTENS AND CORRECTS YOU, for his punishment is proof of his love. Just as a father punishes a child, he delights in to make him better, so the Lord corrects you. (Proverbs 3:11 TLB)

Remember:

Stop fearing or resenting God's correction. He loves you!

Chapter 6: Do not Be Afraid

Proverbs 3:25 (NKJV) - Do not be afraid of sudden terror.

FEAR CAN COME SUDDENLY. An accident, a doctor's diagnosis, an angry quarrel, or a tragedy can trigger panic. Don't let fear paralyze you!

I was diagnosed with clinical depression. How did that happen? An aunt that I loved dearly had recently died, and I asked for temporary help to deal with the loss I was feeling.

I went to my new family doctor, poured out my heart to him, and told him my whole pitiful history of nervousness and insecurity. That was a big mistake!

He said he was glad to help me deal with my aunt's death, and after a lengthy conference lasting 2 OR 3 MINUTES, diagnosed me with clinical depression and prescribed a medication.

The episode was terrifying for me! When I left his office, I was much more depressed and panicky than before. The medicine he prescribed was so strong I could not safely drive my car when I took it. The experience was so distasteful I never went back to that doctor again.

Terror and panic can be crippling. If you have never been through a panic attack, you won't understand it. Lack of knowledge about how to handle different types of problems will make you vulnerable to fear.

Learn to take charge of your own physical and mental well-being! Get back to basics. Are you getting the necessary nutrition, rest, and hydration? Are you refreshing your mind by doing things you enjoy?

Are you getting the proper vitamins and minerals? Are you drinking pure water? Do you rest well at night? Do you take time to truly relax? God loves you and He wants you to take care of yourself!

He can keep you from being overcome by fear and problems. God's love will shield you! His righteousness will form a wall of protection around you! He is your Rock. He is your Fortress! (Psalm 18:2)

We accept God's love for us and walk in that love. God's perfect love casts out fear! There is absolutely no fear in love! You can be assured that His love surrounds you night and day.

Nothing, By Any Means

I had been taught to sink down and be "patient" under the weight of problems; that kind of patience is really resignation. God taught me to stand up and go forward. I stopped avoiding places I feared and started loving and forgiving people who scared me.

I learned to pray for them. That required building good character. If feelings of fear ever came, I stood on my Bible-based authority until they had ended.

Diligence to study the word of God helped in this because the word of God pushed out fearful thoughts. The more I filled my mind with the Bible, the less other things bothered me. I became stronger and more balanced.

In Luke 10:19 Jesus says, "nothing shall by any means hurt you." That is a strong statement! "Nothing, by any means" covers everything!

All evil, all danger, all sickness, all pain, and all destruction results from the fall of man. God didn't create any of it and you don't have to be subject to it. The entire verse says, "Behold, I give unto you power to tread on serpents and scorpions, and over all the power of the enemy: and nothing shall by any means hurt you." "Serpents and scorpions" refers to distinct types of devils. Even death itself is included in the scope of Jesus' words!

Look at Psalm 27:1-3 (AMPC).

1. The Lord is my Light and my Salvation—whom shall I fear or dread? The Lord is the Refuge and Stronghold of my life—of whom shall I be afraid?
2. When the wicked, even my enemies and my foes, came upon me to eat up my flesh, they stumbled and fell.
3. Though a host encamp against me, my heart shall not fear; though war arise against me, [even then] in this will I be confident.

The Lord is a Protector. He shelters from all types of danger and hurtful things. He will even deliver kings into your hand. (Deuteronomy 7:24)

Trust God

Put your trust in God directly. It is God Himself Who will protect you! Many scriptures declare this:

Psalm 91:1-2 (ICB)
Those who go to God Most High for safety
will be protected by God All-Powerful.
I will say to the Lord, "You are my place of safety and protection.
You are my God, and I trust you."

Psalm 46:1-2
God is our refuge and strength,
A very present help in trouble.
Therefore we will not fear,
Even though the earth be removed,
And though the mountains be carried into the midst of the sea.

Hebrews 13:5-6 (ICB)

God has said, "I will never leave you; I will never abandon you." So we can feel sure and say, "I will not be afraid because the Lord is my helper.

Deuteronomy 31:6

Be strong and of a good courage, fear not, nor be afraid of them: for the LORD thy God, he it is that doth go with thee; he will not fail thee, nor forsake thee.

Psalm 118:6

People can't do anything to me.

Protection from Sickness

Psalm 91:6-7 (ICB)

You will not be afraid of diseases that come in the dark
or sickness that strikes at noon.
At your side 1,000 people may die,
or even 10,000 right beside you.
But you will not be hurt.

Strength

Isaiah 40:31 (NKJV) is one of the most well-known Bible verses about strength:

But those who wait on the Lord
Shall renew their strength;
They shall mount up with wings like eagles,
They shall run and not be weary,
They shall walk and not faint.

This verse speaks of His willingness to give strength. He gives power to the weak. Those who wait on Him shall renew their strength and mount up with spiritual "wings" as eagles. We understand the eagle to be a symbol of strength and independence.

God promises can give you strength. Even if you fall, He will get you back up. Proverbs 24:16 (NKJV) says, "For a righteous man may fall seven times and rise again."

The human spirit was never meant to be empty. Don't give up parts of your soul to shame, fear, guilt, and unforgiveness. If you do, you won't have as much room left for praise, thanksgiving, love, or peace.

Fill your mind with the word of God and it will drive out the negatives. Be led by His word and by peace. Ephesians 3:19 is a prayer: "To know the love of Christ which passes knowledge; that you may be filled with all the fullness of God."

Love, Not Fear

I spent years being afraid. Fear drained my energy and overpowered my thoughts. I didn't know how to get rid of fear. I had to learn that perfect love casts out fear!
I John 4:18 (AMPC) says, "There is no fear in love [dread does not exist], but full-grown (complete, perfect) love turns fear out of doors and expels every trace of terror! For fear brings with it the thought of punishment, and [so] he who is afraid has not reached the full maturity of love [is not yet grown into love's complete perfection]."
Someone said, "What if my love is not perfect?" In reality, nothing we do in our own strength will be perfect. His love is perfect!

Ephesians 5:1-2 says: Therefore, be imitators of God as dear children. And walk in love. God will never use fear to correct you or to teach you. Fear is not an instrument of learning. People learn best when they are curious and engaged; they learn nothing when they are afraid. You can overcome all fear as you listen to and obey God's word.

II Timothy 1:7 (NKJV) says: "For God has not given us a spirit of fear, but of power and of love and of a sound mind." God doesn't want you to be afraid. Fear serves no useful purpose in your life. Everything you do must be based on your trust for God.

We see that fear is a spirit. It can come as mere human timidity; the devil can also energize it as he brings more and more tormenting thoughts.

How can you manage thoughts? Take authority over fearful thoughts in the name of Jesus.

If they are demonic in origin, know that the devil is absolutely and always subject to His name! If thoughts are not demonic, then fear can be overcome by learning and applying the word of God.

Whatever cannot be overcome by learning and bearing fruit of the spirit is demonic. Speak directly to fear. Quote scriptures about Jesus' victory and about freedom from fear!

Terror and panic attacks can keep a person paralyzed. How can you deal with things like these? No one can see fear coming and no one can outthink panic. It requires more than mere logic and reasoning.

Learn to Confess Fear

When you feel afraid, confess your fears to God. Keep repeating this action again and again. As you consistently turn from fear to God you will see grow healthier and more rested. Speak all the truths of God concerning healing!

Jesus deals with the greatest fears we have. For me, it was fear of criticism and ridicule. I was fearful of my nosy, acid-tongued relatives living next door! If I stepped outside, they ran to talk to me, and all their conversations were put-downs. They were bullies!

Proverbs 4:16 talks about critical people, "For they sleep not, except they have done mischief; and their sleep is taken away, unless they cause some to fall." Criticism is like food to them. When their victim becomes discouraged, they gossip about her.

Fear is a heavy weight. A renewed mind must look to God and say, "Lord, I put You first! I want to obey You! I trust You!"

Fear makes people self-centered. They put themselves and their fears first. They will do anything to avoid the thing they are afraid of. Check your motives; if they have been selfish, change them. The Bible provides answers to all major fears; This is how it addresses some of them:

Fear of Rejection

God doesn't want you to be afraid of rejection. Ephesians 1:6 says we are accepted in the beloved. Romans 1:7 assures us that God is our Father: "Grace to you and peace from God our Father and the Lord Jesus Christ."

Once you have been born again, all your past sins have been dropped into God's "sea of forgetfulness." If you want to walk in kingdom privilege and dominion, put off the old man. As you do, you will begin to enjoy dominion over your own life.

If you are looking for acceptance, you won't find it very often in this fallen world. There will always be those who reject you. Their questions and ridicule hurt. Why listen to them?

In fleeing rejection, in the blind and headlong pursuit of acceptance, we do all kinds of crazy things. We neglect our health. We make bad decisions, engage in worthless and even harmful activities, and make friends with vile, reprobate people.

Escaping rejection becomes a way of life. People will do almost anything to avoid it. They join themselves to anyone who will accept them. The desire to avoid rejection becomes a major part of their decision-making process.

God will always accept you if you come in Jesus' name. Jesus has made a way, paid the price, and satisfied God's justice.

So, don't waste time fleeing rejection. Concentrate on God's loving acceptance! Jesus was rejected so you could be accepted by God.

Some people will reject you no matter what you do. Stop trying to please them. Just make sure you treat others as you want to be treated. He has said, I will never leave thee, nor forsake thee. (Hebrews 13:5)

Fear of Death

Psalm 23:4 says, "Yea, though I walk through the valley of the shadow of death, I will fear no evil: for thou art with me."

This verse contains an interesting concept. David is going through the valley of the shadow of death but has no fear or awe of it. The word translated "fear" means "to be in awe of, to respect, to dread, to terrify." He is not astonished by the shadow of death and has no terror of it.

In John 5:24 Jesus said, "Verily, verily, I say unto you, He that heareth my word, and believeth on him that sent me, hath everlasting life, and shall not come into condemnation; but is passed from death unto life."

Why? It is because the Lord is with us! Those who believe in Jesus have passed from death to life. We will never see death! John 8:51 - Verily, verily, I say unto you, If a man keeps my saying, he shall never see death.

Fear of People

Do not be afraid of people! Psalm 118:6 says, "The LORD is on my side; I will not fear: what can man do unto me?"

In Isaiah 51:12-13 (NKJV) teaches:

"I, even I, am He who comforts you.
Who are you that you should be afraid
Of a man who will die,
And of the son of a man who will be made like grass?
13 And you forget the LORD your Maker,
Who stretched out the heavens
And laid the foundations of the earth;
You have feared continually every day
Because of the fury of the oppressor,
When he has prepared to destroy.
And where is the fury of the oppressor?

God can take the anger and fury of people and make it evaporate. They may threaten, but God will protect you.

Look at this promise from Isaiah 54:17. "No weapon formed against you shall prosper, And every tongue which rises against you in judgment You shall condemn. This is the heritage of the servants of the LORD, And their righteousness is from Me," Says the LORD.

Mental Torment

The devil wants to torment and drive people with fear, pressure, and guilt. He wants to make them fretful about what may happen in the future. This torment can only be overcome by trust in God's goodness and faithfulness.

Hebrews 13:8 says, "Jesus Christ the same yesterday, and today, and forever." Once you internalize the fact that Jesus will never change, you will begin to understand His love and faithfulness.

I must repeat I John 4:18 (NKJV). It says, "There is no fear in love; but perfect love casts out fear, because fear involves torment. But he who fears has not been made perfect in love." God loves us and we are secure in His love!

No matter what fears may assault you now, you can overcome them with God's word and God's love!

The Joy of the Lord

Our joy is really surety that our Lord Jesus can never fail; our faith is really certainty that God's word is true. This certainty reaches secures whatever we need from God, and His promises are there for us!

The joy of the Lord is our strength! (Neh. 8:10) This indicates that we are to have more than just a joyful spirit, although that is extremely important.

The joy of the Lord is really an unshakable CERTAINTY that He is utterly DEPENDABLE and TRUSTWORTHY.

If Jesus were going to fail, He would have failed on the way to the cross. He humbled Himself to the death of the cross and declared to God "Thy will be done." He did not fail! He remained steadfast!

If He did not fail then, He will not fail in anything else. So, we can trust Him in every area of our lives. This deep and abiding assurance brings joy. It is the joy of the Lord, or joy in the Lord!

The Lord Himself, with all His faithfulness, is our strength! This brings great joy! THE LORD is the One with Who established the New Covenant, and He is at the center of all its promises:

- In Him all things consist.
  Colossians 1:17
- He is Author of faith. Hebrews 12:2
- He is the Head of the church. Ephesians 1:22
- He is our Great High Priest. Hebrews 2:17

He Holds All Things Hold Together

Sometimes people say, "My life is falling apart." That is because their life is not joined to anything stable.

The wicked are like the chaff which the wind blows away. Why? It is because they lack the power and stability of Jesus Christ. Read Colossians 1:17: "And he is before all things, and by him all things consist." So, Jesus Christ is the One Who holds everything together. For Him, all things have been created; everything in life is to serve His purposes.

Since the wicked do not live according to His word, their plans will fall by the wayside and crumble. At the end of his life, my dad was a broken man. I was able to forgive him and help him. We were able to reestablish a loving father-daughter relationship and he accepted Jesus as his Savior!

Help in Crisis

The Lord is watching over you and He knows what you need. The Living Bible says: "For the eyes of the Lord search back and forth across the whole earth, looking for people whose hearts are perfect toward him, so that he can show his great power in helping them."

Here are some other meanings of the Hebrew word "shalem" which was translated "perfect" in this verse: complete, safe, peaceful, whole, full, finished, unharmed.

It can also mean "keeping covenant relation." It refers to those who know how to walk in God's covenant and carries the idea of spiritual maturity. Spiritually mature people know how to rely on God and remain peaceful in crisis.

When bad news comes, trust in Him! Ask for the help you need. Jeremiah 33:3 (GNT) says: "Call to me, and I will answer you; I will tell you wonderful and marvelous things that you know nothing about." The King James Version says: "Call unto me, and I will answer thee, and show thee great and mighty things." "Great" means "large in power and importance." "Mighty" means "secrets and mysteries to make you strong and safe."

We have legal access to the mysteries of God. You cannot totally escape trouble or the challenges of life, but God's provides a "buffer zone" around you that will shield you.

The mark of a believer's strength and faith is the ability to remain calm during trouble and to listen for the voice of the Holy Spirit. Instruction will come. While you are waiting, you can be resting securely in His love. Isaiah 54:14 says, "In righteousness you shall be established; You shall be far from oppression, for you shall not fear; And from terror, for it shall not come near you."

When you are caught in a situation and don't know what to do, have the fruit of the spirit. Have love, joy, peace, and patience. Have kindness, goodness, gentleness, faithfulness, and self-control! DO NOT BE AFRAID OF SUDDEN TERROR, Nor of trouble from the wicked when it comes. (Proverbs 3:25 NKJV)

Remember:

Stop being afraid! Learn to hold yourself calm and wait for God's help. Live in God's protection and comfort.

Chapter 7: Goodness

Proverbs 3:27 (ICB) - Whenever you are able, do good to people who need help.

WE WANT GOD TO BE GOOD TO US, BUT DO WE WANT TO BE GOOD TO OTHERS?

When I was hurting, I didn't want to be kind. After all, I was going through so much! Why should I care about anybody else? They should be doing something to help me!

Like many people, I became used to masquerading and play-acting my way through life. If a lie seems more useful than the truth, I told a lie! What about getting what we want? Does wishing for something hard enough justify any means to get it?

God sees everything and knows everything. Proverbs 15:3 (GNT) makes this clear: "The LORD sees what happens everywhere; God looks at our actions and motives, and His plan is for us to be good, to be sincere and truthful.

Understanding this is an important part of spiritual growth. God's standard is truth, love, and goodness.

What if we can't live up to that? He makes His strength available to us so we will be able to overcome our own immaturity and weaknesses. The Psalmist prayed, "See if there is any bad thing in me. Lead me in the way you set long ago." (Psalm 139:4 ICB)

God's plan is for us to become mature and to help others. He wants everyone to be rescued, to be well, and to have plenty. He doesn't want anyone to suffer. Look at the Garden of Eden. There was no suffering there when He created it.

God's Good Plan

WHAT ARE YOU REACHING FOR? It may surprise you to know that God has a good life planned for you! Jeremiah 29:11 says, "For I know the plans I have for you, says the Lord, to give you a future and a hope."

Ephesians 2:10 (AMPC) says, "For we are God's [own] handiwork (His workmanship), recreated in Christ Jesus, [born anew] that we may do those good works which God predestined (planned beforehand) for us [taking paths which He prepared ahead of time], that we should walk in them [living the good life which He prearranged and made ready for us to live]."

God didn't put you here to suffer; He put you here to love others, to help, and to overcome evil with good. How are we able to do those things? All the good that was due to sinless Jesus has been given to us, and our iniquity with its evil consequences was put upon Him.

Hope

You will never really get well without God's help. Only He can heal the past and give real hope for the future.

Perhaps you feel frozen by memories of the past. Maybe you have been crushed by problems. Depression has worn you out, and hope is hard to find. God's hope is the only real hope.

Hope becomes a target you can aim for with your faith. But what if your need, your situation, is really BIG? You can set smaller targets along the way to your massive main goal.

Hope deferred makes the heart sick. (Proverbs 13:12) The VOICE translation says, "Hope postponed grieves the heart; but when a dream comes true, life is full and sweet." If you have been hoping for something for a long time, it can make you sad when it doesn't come. Learn to place your hopes on Jesus Who can never fail you.

He gives strength! It is not too late. Faith is always now! God will raise your sights to ask bigger because He wants to direct your hope and set it on something great. Because we believe God wants something good for us, we speak about what we are hoping for.

You must believe He is good! Center on the fact that God is good and that He will answer prayer. Daniel 11:32 says, "The people that do know their God shall be strong and do exploits." The implication is that knowing God makes you strong. We know He is good! The essence of Luke 11:13 is that God gives good things to those who ask Him.

Spirit, Soul, and Body

You are an eternal spirit. You will live on forever!

You have a soul which is made of your mind, will, and emotions. You live in a body. This is the "you" people see.

Your mind can be renewed, your will can be changed, and your emotions can be brought under control. The Bible calls your mind, will, and emotions your "soul." In order to be healthy and contented you must give attention to all three parts of your soul.

Your Mind

God's thoughts are different than ours. They are higher! Some people ignore God's thoughts because they don't seem logical according to natural logic. (Isaiah 55:7-9)

Learn God's thoughts by learning His word. He shares them with you! Retrain your mind to think God's thoughts. The Bible tells you what to think about.

Philippians 4:8 says, "Finally, brethren, whatever things are true, whatever things are noble, whatever things are just, whatever things are pure, whatever things are lovely, whatever things are of good report, if there is any virtue and if there is anything praiseworthy—meditate on these things."

Many people have trouble keeping their thoughts on good and lovely things. Past hurts and past wrongs take up all their time. They seem to be wandering through a dark and murky world, complaining every step of the way.

If you have not been walking in the truth, God's word will lead you to hear, to see, and to learn sound teaching.

You don't need "extraordinary faith." Just keep trusting Him to help you! The more your mind is renewed, the less mental pressure you will have. Be afraid of no one! Despise no one, but don't value any one person too much.

Be transformed by the renewing of your mind. Say what the Bible says. Humble yourself and accept what the word of God says. Prove what is the good, acceptable, and perfect will of God.

Your Will

God is after your will, your motives because He wants to change your goals and your direction.

Do you know the will of God for your life? He wants you to turn from pain, destruction, and fear and turn towards healing, wholeness, and peace!

People shy away from church and from God because they don't want to be corrected. God does not want to scold you; He wants to heal you!

Now you know God is on your side; which direction will you go? Where is your life headed? What motivates you? What are you striving for?

Back when I chose my own direction, little problems sidetracked me. I couldn't seem to keep going on one heading very long.

I was confused and frustrated. Maybe you are too. Really, there is only one choice. Will you go towards God or away from Him?

God has a solution for you. Psalm 50:23 says, "He who offers a sacrifice of praise and thanksgiving honors Me; And to him who orders his way rightly [who follows the way that I show him], I shall show the salvation of God."

When you start to live life in the way He directs, His supernatural saving power will begin to lift you up!

Your Emotions

Feelings are emotions, and you don't have to let them run your life! Your spirit, guided by the Holy Spirit, should be in charge. Keep your feelings under control; stop letting feelings control you!

Don't allow emotions to be affected by a sense of frustration. Decide what you are going to do. You can say, "I am not going to be angry. I am not going to be afraid."

If your emotions are out of control, you may not seem to have any choice other than being upset. If that sounds like your life, ask God's help. He will perform a rescue for you. Psalm 40:1-3 (TLB) says:

1. I waited patiently for God to help me; then he listened and heard my cry.
2. He lifted me out of the pit of despair, out from the bog and the mire, and set my feet on a hard, firm path, and steadied me as I walked along.

He will lift you out of the quicksand of confusion, addiction, or fear, and He will set your feet on an even, solid place so you can go forward. Doubt and delay will be over!

Line up your FEELINGS and EMOTIONS with His word. See what the Bible says. If you choose to remain in the dark, He will never be able to bring you into a broad, open place.

Remember that GOD is GOOD!

Are You Angry?

Do you feel angry? Do you have a right to be angry? What does the Bible say? "If you are angry, don't sin by nursing your grudge. Don't let the sun go down with you still angry—get over it quickly." (Ephesians 4:26 TLB)

Anger is a work of the flesh. Have you used tantrums to get your way? Have you tried to manipulate other people?

These are dangerous seeds to plant. Treat others exactly as you want to be treated. Love everyone and think the best of everyone.

A righteous woman keeps calm in the day of adversity; she doesn't become angry or talk back. She keeps her heart from forming a grudge against those involved in her trouble.

It takes spiritual maturity to stand in a difficult place, allowing God to bring breakthrough in answer to your prayers.

Anger can block you from receiving God's best. A person who is often angry is out of control.

Good sense makes a man restrain his anger, and it is his glory to overlook a transgression or an offense. (Proverbs 19:11 AMPC) We overlook what people do to us and forgive them.

A moderate amount of anger can be useful IF it is directed towards a problem or an injustice. Never direct your anger at people! Can you control anger?

Proverbs says you can: "He that is slow to anger is better than the mighty; and he that rules his spirit than he that takes a city." (Proverbs 16:32)

Are You Offended?

Every Christian has been offended at some point.

Some believers have allowed offense to push them into a season of unbelief. (Unbelief is refusing something you know is true.)

If you can make peace with another person, do it. If it takes an apology from you, then apologize. Forget whose fault it is! God is interested in peace between people. Being right is never more important than that.

Know this: Some people are just angry all the time. People who are easily offended will get mad no matter what you say or do. Forgive them and forget the thing! Don't allow it to stand in the way of your peace and spiritual growth.

I knew a 16-year-old boy who had gotten offended and had absolutely given up on life. He stood in my classroom and told me his mother was an alcoholic, and that because of HER terrible mistakes, his life was OVER. He was offended at his mother!

That boy's mother had hurt him, and he needed to forgive her. Forgiveness and confessing sins are two of God's "pruning tools." God wants to clear out anything that doesn't promote or enhance His life in you.

I prayed silently, "Lord, help me know what to say to encourage him."

I answered, "You don't know that. You can't say your life is over! Keep going! I believe you will do wonderful things. First, you need to forgive her." My words seemed to help, and that young teenage boy left my classroom looking more hopeful.

After he graduated from high school, he joined the military and began a new life. I believe he did forgive her.

Think You Can't Forgive?

Some people say, "I just can't forgive. The things done to me are just too bad." Some acts and words seem too awful to forgive. At least, they do according to human reasoning.

There are no special cases! Things done to you may seem too hard to forgive, but others have suffered as much, and many have suffered more. We have all suffered unjustly in some way. In God's kingdom, we must forgive EVERYTHING, large and small.

In Mark 11:25 (TLB) Jesus says, "But when you are praying, first forgive anyone you are holding a grudge against, so that your Father in heaven will forgive you your sins too."

Unforgiveness creates spiritual hang-ups you don't need. The enemy will use unforgiveness to bring confusion, uncertainty, strife, and fear. Are you praying for help from God? Forgive!

Are You Envious?

Proverbs 27:4 (GW) says, "Anger is cruel, and fury is overwhelming,

but who can survive jealousy?"

You may admire some people and envy others. You may think you deserve what they have more than they do!

God offers His blessings generously to everyone! They are there whenever you seek them, so you should never envy anyone else.

Be grateful for everything! Never feel sorry for yourself! God needs you to walk with Him and be involved in your own blessing process. It is a partnership!

God's Plan

There is no way to look ahead and know what God can do in your future. He can't always tell you because His plans are too wonderful and complex. You will have to trust Him to make the right choices for you.

Don't panic! God can get you into any opportunity that is good and out of any situation that is harmful. Seeing those around you make snap judgments may tempt you to make snap judgments too. Remember who you are in Christ. Expect circumstances to turn in your favor.

Psalm 37:23-24 (AMPC) The steps of a [good] man are directed and established by the Lord when He delights in his way [and He busies Himself with his every step]. Though he falls, he shall not be utterly cast down, for the Lord grasps his hand in support and upholds him.

We do not always see God's plan at first. "Man's steps are ordered and ordained by the LORD. How then can a man [fully] understand his way?" (Proverbs 20:24) "But the path of the just is as the shining light, that shineth more and more unto the perfect day." (Proverbs 4:8)

Be Generous!

Goodness is a fruit of the spirit, and it centers on helping others. Do you desire to be good like Jesus is? Then go ahead and be good! You can draw on His goodness and spend it on others! His tender mercies are over all His works!

Jesus wants us to be generous and give! We can give time or money to others. We can pray for someone else. Even kind words can be like gifts. As we enrich the lives of others our own lives will benefit.

Be generous with forgiveness! Don't dwell on the faults and missteps of those around you. Forgive them and forget them. Be glad when others are rewarded or promoted. Don't strive for position.

Luke 6:30 (TLB)

Give what you have to anyone who asks you for it; and when things are taken away from you, don't worry about getting them back.

Proverbs 11:24 (MSG) - The world of the generous gets larger and larger.

In II Corinthians 9:7 Paul describes how we are to give to God's work: Let each one [give] as he has made up his own mind and purposed in his heart, not reluctantly or sorrowfully or under compulsion, for God loves (He takes pleasure in, prizes above other things, and is unwilling to abandon or to do without) a cheerful (joyous, "prompt to do it") giver [whose heart is in his giving]. (AMPC)

Honor Father and Mother

We are commanded to honor father and mother. This is a commandment with promise. Exodus 20:12 says, "Honor your father and your mother, that your days may be long upon the land which the LORD your God is giving you."

But what if you don't believe your parents deserve honor? No matter what you think of them, God wants you to honor them. Forgive them if you have anything against them. Treat them with respect. No matter how old you are, honor your parents. This will produce a significant effect on you and on them, and God will bless you for doing what He says!

God's Answers

God wants your questions to be answered. He has packed the Bible full of answers for you. Sometimes, because God is so great, His wisdom so vast, His will so perfect, and His heart so magnificent, His answers come in the form of sweeping statements about Himself. He IS the answer!

- If you want love, God is love. I John 4:8
- If you have needs, God is faithful. I Cor. 1:9
- If you lack wisdom, God supplies it. James 1:5
- If you are afraid, God's love casts it out. I John 4:18

Match your need to His answer and His supply. To have the mind of Christ is to understand Christ's motives and actions as set forth in the New Testament. When you have the mind of Christ, you will be able to understand Him more fully.

One of Christ's roles is Burden Bearer. You want God to be involved in your life, in every step you take. You want Him to bear your burdens.

You want Him to help you and bless you, so have the mind of Christ! Do good for others. "Withhold not good from them to whom it is due, when it is in the power of thine hand to do it." (Proverbs 3:27)

Each time you participate in exercise your body gets stronger and each time you overcome evil with good your spirit gets stronger. Good is a strong force because it comes from God. It is strong enough to overcome the evils of this world.

How do you recognize God's presence? When His presence comes on the scene you will begin to worship. You will know He is good!

So do as much good for others as you can. Be helpful and generous. When you do this, you are acting like your Father in heaven. He is good!

Remember:

Do good to others whenever you get a chance. Kind deeds large and small will be noticed and rewarded by God.

Chapter 8: Guard Your Heart

Proverbs 4:23 (GW) - Guard your heart more than anything else, because the source of your life flows from it.

I WAS ALWAYS TOO OPEN WITH PEOPLE because I was seeking their approval. I was chasing acceptance from those around me like some individuals run after success. But the satisfaction I hoped to gain from approval was always just out of reach; it was always somewhere ahead of me.

People around me were always judging, approving, or disapproving of everything I did. I didn't have the life skills necessary to block judgmental words and glances.

John 12:43 (AMP) says, "They loved the approval of men more than the approval of God." That perfectly describes the way I was thinking.

No one had ever explained to me that I could get approval from God Himself. The Bible plainly says we can!

Hebrews 11:39 lists people in the Old Testament who "gained [divine] approval through their faith."

Some of these are Noah, Abraham, Sarah, Isaac, Jacob, Joseph, Moses, Gideon, Samson, and David.

By having faith, you can gain God's approval! Once you know you have God's favor, the approval of people won't seem so important.

Some in your circle will accept you even while others reject you. Refuse to worry about it!

People are always changing while God remains the same. God has a good plan for your life. Set your focus on that!

God keeps filling our lives with blessings until past hurts are forgotten. His mercy is enough. His forgiveness is enough. His faith is enough. His love is enough.

Focus on the marvelous gifts He gives and mark this as a new beginning in your life.

God's blessings can overtake you and blot out past pain. This happens as you learn to keep your heart from being hurt, afraid, or bitter.

Don't Be Too Open

The Bible teaches us about protecting ourselves within well-placed boundaries.

A story from Song of Solomon describes big brothers watching out for a little sister. They don't want her to be too open with strangers.

"If she be a wall, we will build upon her a palace of silver: and if she be a door, we will enclose her with boards of cedar." (Solomon 8:9)

They wanted their sister to be careful who she spent time with. They didn't want her to open up her heart like a door! They didn't want her to tell others her feelings.

They wanted her to guard her heart and to put up a "wall" around her emotions. Proverbs 4:23 (TLB) says, "Above all else, guard your affections, for they influence everything else in your life."

Too much openness to the world is not a good thing. Being too open with people marks you as immature, thoughtless, naïve, and vulnerable.

It can slow down what the Holy Spirit is trying to do in your life. Listen to the Holy Spirit's leading! You may need to set yourself apart from some people. If they are speaking fear or toxic words, you don't need much contact with them. They won't care what you think or feel, and it will leave you vulnerable later. Only confide in your closest loved ones.

- Take control over your own life.
- Don't allow thoughts of fear in your mind.
- Guard your heart from bitterness and hatred.

God wants His covenant to keep you separated from the world and safe. If you want this type of protection, carefully guard who you let into your life.

Jesus should be at the center of all you do! Colossians 1:17 (AMP) says: "In Him all things hold together." Ever feel like you are falling apart? Place Jesus at the center of your life!

Covenant Minded

The New Testament is a blood-sworn covenant, or oath between Father God and Jesus Christ.

If we walk in the provisions of that covenant, we can inherit ALL the blessings God has provided for us and promised us.

Jesus established the New Covenant. It was the plan of God to send Him to heal the brokenhearted and release the oppressed. Jesus is the Lord; He never changes! It is comforting to realize He came to set us free.

Isaiah 61:1 says, "The Spirit of the Lord GOD is upon Me, Because the LORD has anointed Me To preach good tidings to the poor; He has sent Me to heal the brokenhearted, To proclaim liberty to the captives, And the opening of the prison to those who are bound."

Jesus announced His mission on earth in Luke 4:18: "The Spirit of the LORD is upon Me, Because He has anointed Me To preach the gospel to the poor; He has sent Me to heal the brokenhearted, To proclaim liberty to the captives And recovery of sight to the blind, To set at liberty those who are oppressed."

Fiery, Undeserved trials

Unexpected, undeserved trials break the will of so many Christians because they feel betrayed.

I Peter 4:12 says, "Beloved, think it not strange concerning the fiery trial which is to try you, as though some strange thing happened unto you."

Do you feel that you have been unfairly targeted or misused? Betrayal by a close friend can push someone completely off track. Don't think this is strange! Thieves and killers come suddenly. They pounce! The devil is a thief and a destroyer.

Words can infect people with bitterness. A tongue can be a dangerous weapon.

Can you bear the fruit of love and patience when people are not treating you fairly? When other Christians refuse to forgive, can you still love them?

Fight the Good Fight of Faith

Depression can be more than mere thoughts. It can be an indication you are dealing with a negative spiritual force. Are you giving place to the presence of the enemy? Take authority over it! Cast down negative thoughts. II Corinthians 10:4 says, "For the weapons of our warfare are not carnal, but mighty through God to the pulling down of strong holds."

The devil is a spirit being, and we cannot deal with him in the natural realm. Unforgiveness, hatred, and jealousy can be strongholds. Jealousy can be a way of saying "poor me!" Love and forgiveness can break these sorts of strongholds. Love and forgive others and confess your own faults.

Is there someone in your life that you cannot forgive? You may say, "I can't talk to anyone about this; it is too personal, and it hurts too much to forgive." Jesus has done His part; He has defeated and disarmed the devil. Now, we must do our part, which is to forgive anyone we have anything against.

When something seems terribly unfair, people think: "I cannot forgive that! I can't see a way out of this problem. I feel trapped." Unforgiveness is a sin. Like sins you repented of when you got saved, you must drop it. You have been redeemed and set free!

You may feel that your weaknesses, physical, emotional, and even spiritual, will keep you down for the rest of your life. They don't have to! Yes, we are sometimes weak, but God has given us His strength.

We can cover the weaknesses of others.

Some families cooperate so beautifully that you can hardly tell where one person's contributions leave off and another's begin.

That is how God wants to cooperate with you. He freely offers His strength and His wisdom. They are always available, and you never have to function without them again! Remember that quietness plus confidence equals strength. (Isaiah 30:15, 32:17-18)

When two people argue they are operating in strife. Strife drives each of them to insist on his or her way. Strife insists on winning!

Strife

How can you stay out of strife? Don't answer back when someone else starts to argue. What if you believe the other person is wrong and you are right? Staying out of strife and backbiting is much more important than being right. Proverbs 20:3 (MSG) teaches, "Fools love to pick fights."

Strife is dangerous too. James 3:16 says, "For where envying and strife is, there is confusion and every evil work."

Do you really want confusion and evil in your life? Of course not! So, refuse to be involved in strife.

Overcome Evil with Good

Romans 12:21 says, "Be not overcome of evil, but overcome evil with good."

Divorce, death of a loved one, failure, or disappointed hopes can cause pain that won't go away. These events can cause trauma, and trauma requires years and years to heal; it can overshadow all your good memories. Depressed people may feel that they have lost every good thing from their lives.

Sometimes good memories become painful because they are so closely linked to bad ones. Who wants to remember birthdays or Christmas celebrations which included members of the family who are now absent? It is much easier and far less painful not to remember at all!

It is possible to recover your good memories!

- Forgive people who have wounded you.
- Ask forgiveness for things you have done.

- Ask God to help you reclaim good memories that have been lost.
- Ask God to heal you from bad experiences.

Believe those loved ones who died went on to a better place. Even people who did not appear to be saved may have accepted Christ in their last moments. If you ever called their name over in prayer, believe that He saved them.

Love and Forgive

Often people don't love and forgive because they don't believe they can. This is the devil's lie. We can love others because God pours His love into our hearts.

Romans 5:5 says, "And hope makes not ashamed; because the love of God is shed abroad in our hearts by the Holy Ghost which is given unto us." We can love others with God's own love. We can forgive them because we have been forgiven.

Believers in Jesus must forgive! Mark 11:25-26 says:

25 And when ye stand praying, forgive, if ye have ought against any: that your Father also which is in heaven may forgive you your trespasses.
26 But if ye do not forgive, neither will your Father which is in heaven forgive your trespasses.

If we refuse to forgive others, God will not forgive us. God wants us to choose forgiveness, but many people choose unforgiveness instead. Unforgiveness will dominate your thinking if you let it. If you have been wronged by someone, that person's name or image may seem to torment you.

Once you have confessed hatred, bitterness, grudges, and even worry to God, He will begin to solve those problems.

God is Not Religious

Are you trying to use religious methods to get an answer from God? Remember that God is not religious-minded; rather, He is covenant minded. He has provided everything you need within the New Covenant.

II Peter 1:3 (GW) - God's divine power has given us everything we need for life and for godliness. This power was given to us through knowledge of the one who called us by his own glory and integrity.

God has already given everything you need. Discover and use the appropriate Bible verses. His own integrity is center stage!

- He cleanses you. I John 1:7,9
- He gives you grace. James 4:6
- He gives strength. II Cor. 12:9
- He answers prayer. Jas. 1:5-6; Heb. 11:6; Mat. 21:21-22
- He gives help in temptation. Hebrews 2:18
- He provides peace. Philippians 4:7
- He supplies needs. Philippians 4:19

Don't listen to songs about HEARTACHE, LOSS, SUICIDE, or DEATH. Refuse to watch movies about rejection, fear, or betrayal. If you do, your mind will dwell on those things. Instead, think on good and lovely things. No trauma is bigger than God Who lives outside of time and space. He is Lord of all, and He will help you.

New Testament Portraits of Christians:

Dear children - Keep your eyes on God and act like He acts. Dear children watch their father and do what he does.

Be ye therefore followers of God,
as dear children; and walk in love… (Ephesians 5:1)

Athletes - Be as patient as an athlete in training. "Let us run with patience the race that is set before us." (Hebrews 12:1)

Golden vessels – Golden vessels are too honorable to hold gossip, jealousy, bitterness, or any such thing.

Become the kind of container God can use to present any and every kind of gift to his guests for their blessing. (II Timothy 2:21 MSG)

Fruitful branches - Branches can bear fruit if they stay connected to the vine. Without that connection, they wither. Jesus is the Vine, and we are the branches. He wants us to bear much fruit!

"I am the vine; you are the branches. He who abides in Me, and I in him, bears much fruit; for without Me you can do nothing. John 15:5 (NKJV)

What Must You Overcome?

- We overcome the world. 1 John 5:4
- We overcome evil with good. Romans 12:21
- We overcome the wicked one. John 2:14
- We overcome those who judge us. Isaiah 54:17

Enforce Your Peace

You must know that your feet are shod with the preparation of the gospel of peace, and that makes you able to take AUTHORITY over what causes chaos in your life.

Jesus defeated every foe to bring His peace to us. It is more than just assurance that we are saved. It is victory in every part of our earthly lives.

Being "shod with the preparation of the Gospel of peace" means you are clothed with the "shalom" Jesus bought for you, "the peace that passes all understanding."

What is the peace of God that passes understanding? It is peace that this world cannot comprehend. It is total peace. In order to experience this, you must become the enforcer of your own peace using the name of Jesus. You can understand it because you have the mind of Christ.

Meditate on scriptures about peace throughout the day. Jesus purchased it for you, and you can have it. Wherever you are and whatever you are doing, expect to be in peace.

Pursue peace - Seek peace and pursue it. (Psalm 34:14) So, let's pursue those things which bring peace. (Romans 14:19 GW) Pursue peace with everyone. (Hebrews 12:14)

Be led by peace - For you shall go out with joy and be led out with peace. (Isaiah 55:12 NKJV)

In Joshua 1:3 God says, "Every place that the sole of your foot shall tread upon, that have I given unto you, as I said unto Moses."

The Hebrew word translated "tread upon" means "to tread, march forth, to tread a bow." In other words, Joshua was to march forward, ready to fight. When he did, victory would follow.

Jesus has already won the victory. When we make a stand in His name, we partake of His victory!

Plan for Peace

"Joy fills hearts that are planning peace!" Proverbs 12:20 (NLT)

Psalm 122:7 says, "Peace be within thy walls." Peace is God's plan for you, and your house should be a peaceful place.

Jesus is the source of your peace:

- The punishment that brought our peace was on him. (Isa. 53:5 WEB)
- For He Himself is our peace. (Eph. 2:14 AMP)
- "And the work of righteousness shall be peace; and the effect of righteousness quietness and assurance forever." (Isaiah 32:17)

Enjoyment

Laughter does you good like medicine! Find something that gives you enjoyment. Rediscover a hobby, game, or sport and learn to love it all over again! Plan for times when you take an hour or two to enjoy your favorite things.

Learn something new! Take up music, sketching, or carpentry. Begin to crochet, do crossword puzzles, or bake. Study your new pursuit and learn all you can about it!

We are commanded not to worry. I Peter 5:7 says, "Casting all your care upon him; for he cares for you." Jesus taught that care, entering in, would choke the word.

One way you can keep from carrying the care of your situation is to have joy. Rejoice in your salvation! Rejoice in the Lord!

Romans 5:11 (TLB) says, "Now we rejoice in our wonderful new relationship with God—all because of what our Lord Jesus Christ has done in dying for our sins—making us friends of God."

You can also rejoice in all the marvelous things God has created! Any sport reflects His handiwork. He invented physics! A tennis ball behaves differently than a football does. A baseball bounces differently than a ping-pong ball. Watching sports can be relaxing too. (Mute the commercials and commentary if they aren't wholesome!)

So, joy deprives worry of mental space. We literally "don't give place to the devil" when we choose joy over worry. What does God's word say about you?

If you are born again, it says much about you:

- You are accepted in the beloved.
  Eph. 1:6
- You have eternal life.
  John 3:15
- You have the righteousness of God.
  Romans 3:22,
- Jesus died on the cross for you.
  I Corinthians 1:18
- He rose again to represent you before God.
  Romans 4:25

You, Yourself

Another thing covenant teaches is that you are important to God. That means He loves you for who you are! Don't try to copy other people. To say you want to be "just like" another person is not helpful. You can't see all their faults and their mistakes.

The Bible's pages are filled with wisdom and knowledge. Until you have internalized that wisdom and knowledge and understand how to apply it, you will continue to make mistakes in judgement.

I used to beg God, "Please help me to not make any more mistakes!" Life is not perfect or ideal, as much as we may want it to be. Remember that He is your rear guard, taking care of your past right up to this moment.

As you repent for what you have done wrong and forgive others for their mistakes, as you learn from the Bible's wisdom, you will make fewer and fewer mistakes. This is the only way we learn and grow. God will encourage you every step of the way! Be the best "you" possible! He created you to be yourself. You can only do that if you guard your heart.

Remember:

GUARD YOUR HEART more than anything else because the source of your life flows from it. (Proverbs 4:23 GW)

Chapter 9: Honor God

Praise the LORD's greatness with me. Let us highly honor his name together. Psalm 34:3 (GW)

BY PRAISING GOD AND HONORING HIS NAME YOU BRING HIM CLOSE. Psalm 100:4 gives us a way to enter His throne room. "Enter into His gates with thanksgiving, And into His courts with praise. Be thankful to Him and bless His name."

To magnify the Lord is to focus on Him and honor Him. See Him as the pivot point of all your decisions. Keep Jesus at the center of your life and at the heart of your thoughts. Keep Him in first place!

If you are going to overcome obstacles, see yourself as living and abiding in God's very presence now, accepted, beloved, and safe.

How can you have this kind of fellowship with God? First, you must be born again. When you accept Jesus Christ as your Savior, you are born again! You are spiritually alive and God's child.

See Him as carrying your sins and taking your punishment. Allow Him to die on the cross in your place.

Then, see Him as resurrected and appearing before God on your behalf, as full assurance of your justification. He has already fulfilled all these things!

He was raised for your (and my) justification. Think of it this way: if Jesus hadn't completely fulfilled all of God's requirements about sin, He would not have been raised from the dead!

Some people are afraid to accept God. For them, He looks like a spiritual crutch. Jesus offers you a COVENANT and not a CRUTCH!

The New Covenant is a blood-sworn oath declaring what He will do for you. Jesus can do what no other person can do for you!

Jesus

- There is no other name through which we can be saved.

"And there is salvation in no one else, for there is no other name under heaven given among men by which we must be saved." (Acts 4:12 ESV)

- There is no other One Who gives faith.
  "Looking unto Jesus, Author and Finisher of our faith" (Hebrews 12:2)

- There is no other One Who forgiveness.
  "Come now, and let us reason together, saith the LORD: though your sins be as scarlet, they shall be as white as snow; though they be red like crimson, they shall be as wool." (Isaiah 1:18)

- There is no other One who can satisfy us.
  "And Jesus said unto them, I am the bread of life: he that cometh to Me shall never hunger; and he that believeth on Me shall never thirst." (John 6:35)

- There is no other One so faithful.

"All that the Father giveth Me shall come to Me; and him that cometh to Me I will in no wise cast out." (John 6:37)

- There is no other way to the Father.

  "Jesus saith unto him, I am the way, the truth, and the life: no man cometh unto the Father, but by Me." (John 14:6)

Author and Champion

Within the word "authority" is "author." Who has the authority to offer us God's plan of salvation? Who has the right to assure us that God will be faithful to help us? Who can tell us to place all our confidence in the New Covenant? Who has proven God's goodness to us? Jesus Christ has!

Hebrews 12:2 (Mounce) says: "Fixing our gaze upon Jesus, the pioneer (archēgon) and perfecter of our faith, who rather than the joy set before him endured a cross, disregarding its shame, and has now taken his seat at the right hand of the throne of God."

William D. Mounce's translation of the New Testament defines "archēgon" as "a CHIEF, a LEADER, a PRINCE, an AUTHOR." In every way, Jesus is our Champion!

The Mounce version of Acts 5:31 says: "God exalted this Jesus to his own right hand as Leader (archēgon) and Savior, so as to provide repentance…and the remission of sins." The Bible is really the story of Jesus. Jesus is called the Word of God. He is the Prince of Peace!

Authorship

Authorship carries the idea of authority. In other words, an author has authority to write. An author can present an insider's view of true events.

Jesus used faith, taught faith, and responds to faith.

Jesus has been where no one else has and He has done what no one else could do. He redeemed us with His own blood.

Because of this, "God also has highly exalted Him [Jesus] and given Him the name which is above every name." (Philippians 2:9 NKJV)

He was given a name above every name. That is how our faith was completed. Hearing *His* word causes faith to come!

Holy Spirit: Comforter and Teacher

One of the ways the Holy Spirit comforts us is to remind us of who we are in Christ. He brings the peace of Christ into our daily lives. Will you let peace rule you? Will you allow the Holy Spirit to comb through every thought, every memory, every attitude now? He will qualify some thoughts as good and disqualify others.

Leave behind feelings of guilt and thoughts of unworthiness. Jesus has made all believers worthy and has made them righteous with His very own righteousness. The Holy Spirit will always remind you of this!

He will teach you how to obey God's instructions in the New Testament. He will relieve your cares if you let Him. He will lead you into all truth.

When He becomes your Teacher, you won't have to rely only on what you are able to figure out for yourself. He will show you what you need to know!

Our Heavenly Father

There is one thing you must understand: God is a heavenly Father, and He has a father's heart. He wants to care for you! If you approach God as a religious experience, you will be disappointed. God wants communication with you! He wants a relationship.

God reveals Himself through His word. That is the principal way we can know Him. And we really can know HIM!

Does God ever engage in an act of destruction? NO! That is foreign to Him. Psalm 103:4 says, "He has redeemed our lives from destruction." He is a Healer and a Restorer.

Hebrews 1:1-2 is a starting point for those who really want to know about God:

"God, who at various times and in various ways spoke in time past to the fathers by the prophets, has in these last days spoken to us by His Son, whom He has appointed heir of all things, through whom also He made the worlds."

If you want to know about God, look at Jesus! Did Jesus destroy or heal? Did He display hate or love? Did He punish or redeem? He showed us the Father's heart. He is the express image of God! Numbers 6:24-26 (TLB) records a blessing: May the Lord bless and protect you; may the Lord's face radiate with joy because of you; may he be gracious to you, show you his favor, and give you his peace.

Trinity

In the Bible, we see the Trinity as three distinct Persons. At the time of Jesus' baptism in the River Jordan, God the Father anointed Him, and the Holy Spirit confirmed His ministry. Jesus was being baptized, the Holy Spirit was descending on Him, and the Father was speaking from heaven.

Matthew 3:16-17: And Jesus, when he was baptized, went up straightway out of the water: and, lo, the heavens were opened unto him, and he saw the Spirit of God descending like a dove, and lighting upon him: And lo a voice from heaven, saying, This is my beloved Son, in whom I am well pleased.

Jesus said only what He heard the Father saying and did only what He saw the Father doing, and He was anointed by the Holy Spirit to do God's work.

Acts 10:38 - God anointed Jesus of Nazareth with the Holy Spirit and with power, who went about doing good and healing all who were oppressed by the devil, for God was with Him.

A Portrait of God

- God cannot lie.
- God honors His word.
- God doesn't change.
- God is compassionate and willing to heal.
- God is love, and His love never fails.

What we believe about God is most important. Likewise, what we believe about ourselves is critical too. In the New Testament, the righteousness Jesus provides us becomes our rest.

Fellowship

Your inner life should be one of beautiful and unbroken fellowship with Him. Talk to Him about your secrets and He will reveal to you His hidden treasures. (Deuteronomy 29:29) He has hidden treasures in His word for believers, but first He wants us to come to Him, believe on Him, and commit our lives to Him.

Once you taste real closeness with God, nothing less will satisfy! You won't be religious, and you will never trust the world's ways again! Together, you and God will go forward. He will satisfy your hunger, and you will know you are walking out His will for YOU!

You will find His best! What is it like to be close to God? God is love! You will be wrapped in His love when you come close to Him. Bless His Name!

Keep God's Name Unique and Holy

1. I bless the holy name of God with all my heart.
2. Yes, I will bless the Lord and not forget the glorious things he does for me.
3. He forgives all my sins. He heals me. (Psalm 103:1-3)

If you have been using God's name to curse, change direction and use His name to bless! You will be blessed as you bless His name and remember His benefits! Don't watch or listen to any type of program in which God's name is cursed!

Make sure to keep God's name holy in your thinking and speaking. Don't use His name as a curse word and don't ridicule it. To respect God's name is to respect Him. He wants you to respect His name; if you respect Him then He can get help to you.

His name can keep you safe. "The name of the LORD is a strong tower: the righteous runs into it and is safe." (Proverbs 18:10)

One of the Ten Commandments warns, "GOD won't put up with the irreverent use of his name." Deut. 5:11 (MSG) The New Living Version says, "Do not use the name of the Lord your God in a bad way. For the Lord will punish the one who uses His name in a bad way."
Psalm 5:11 says, "Let those also who love Your name Be joyful in You." What other name can deliver us? Psalm 8:9 says, "O LORD, our Lord, how excellent is Your name in all the earth!"
Psalm 23:3 says, "He restores my soul; He leads me in the paths of righteousness For His name's sake." Love Him because He is faithful. Love Him because He rescues. Love Him because of His word and because He keeps His covenant.

Love the Lord!

- He gives you His own love. (Romans 5:5)
- He gives you His own peace. (John 14:27)
- He gives you His own faith. (Galatians 2:20)
- He gives you His own joy. (John 15:11)

He will love you and bless you and multiply you. (Deuteronomy 7:13 AMPC) His love is like an ocean; He heals because He loves. Do you believe God loves you? Love created faith and hope for you. Actually, He loves you too much to let you stay sick!

Remember:

Honor the Lord in your own life. Respect Him and listen to Him. Praise Him! He will visit you. He will deliver you. Ask Him to be your Champion!

Chapter 10: All Glorious Within

The ways of right-living people glow with light; the longer they live, the brighter they shine. (Proverbs 4:18 MSG)

WHAT DOES YOUR HEART LOOK LIKE TO GOD? Is it "all glorious" with love for God and love for others? Are you walking on a shining path that grows brighter and brighter?

When you truly know God loves you, you will have no more fear. He said His love would never fail and it casts out fear! God's covenant love is perfect, and it is eternal.

He has made it possible for us to love others because His love has been deposited in our hearts by the Holy Spirit. This is all based on what He did for us first. "He first loved us…"

People have trouble believing it is that simple. They can't believe God really loves them. The story of salvation is so easy that many people overlook it!

God is Good

God is good and all good things come from Him. The Bible's account of creation does not mention any bad things. God did not create death, sickness, tragedy, or poverty. All these things came as the result of Adam's treason which gave Satan dominion over the earth.

God's response to this was to send Jesus. In John 10:10 Jesus says, "The thief cometh not but for to steal, and to kill, and to destroy; I am come that they might have life, and that they might have it more abundantly." Satan brought death, sickness, tragedy, and poverty. Jesus gives us life, health, peace, and abundance!

How Are You Doing?

Are you still feeling sorry for yourself? Are you still desperate and afraid? Are you still begging people to pray? Do you still feel hopeless? Do you still believe your problems are part of God's sovereign plan? You must learn to cast all your cares on Him and rejoice!

What fellowship has light with darkness? You can have fellowship with Jesus! You can walk in the light as He is in the light. Our lives grow brighter and brighter into a perfect day. (Proverbs 4:18) In the Bible, "perfection" means "maturity." That perfect day is not in heaven; it is the mature believer's daily life.

Jesus taught about lighting a candle and He called John the Baptist a torch. The New Testament church is to be filled with light and with all the fulness of His moral excellence. It is to be a glorious church without spot or wrinkle.

God's Love

I Corinthians 13:4-8 (NKJV) paints a portrait of real love:

Love suffers long and is kind; love does not envy; love does not parade itself, is not puffed up; does not behave rudely, does not seek its own, is not provoked, thinks no evil; does not rejoice in iniquity, but rejoices in the truth; bears all things, believes all things, hopes all things, endures all things. Love never fails.

Christ's Love

Paul wrote: [I pray that you] may be able to comprehend with all the saints what is the width and length and depth and height— to know the love of Christ which passes knowledge; that you may be filled with all the fullness of God. [emphasis mine]

We can understand Christ's love by studying His actions in the gospels. He didn't "quench a smoking flax or break a bruised reed."

He always encouraged people! He will never discourage one who is trying. He will never reject one who has grown lukewarm, or one who has made a habit of saying the wrong things, or one who has been damaged. Isaiah 42:3 says: "A bruised reed He will not break, and smoking flax He will not quench; He will bring forth justice for truth."

The Living Bible translates the last part of that verse like this: "He will encourage the fainthearted, those tempted to despair. He will see full justice given to all who have been wronged."

God's Compassion

Compassion is part of God's nature. "But you are merciful and gentle, Lord, slow in getting angry, full of constant loving-kindness and of truth.

(Psalm 86:15 TLB) "GOD is all mercy and grace— not quick to anger, is rich in love." (Psalm 145:8 MSG) Lamentations 3:22 says, "His compassions fail not."

Jesus had compassion. "But when he saw the multitudes, he was moved with compassion on them, because they fainted, and were scattered abroad, as sheep having no shepherd." (Matthew 9:36) Matthew 20:34 describes His healing of blind men. "Jesus had compassion on them and touched their eyes: and immediately their eyes received sight, and they followed him."

Mark 1:41 describes His healing of a leper. "And Jesus, moved with compassion, put forth his hand, and touched him, and saith unto him, 'I will; be thou clean.'"

In the desert, God shaded the Israelites during the daytime with a cloud so they wouldn't get too hot. At night, He was their light, pushing back the darkness for them.

Love is Key

Love is key in God's kingdom. We can show love by being generous. We can show it by being kind, patient, faithful, and by thinking the best of every person.

Jesus asked Peter, "Do you love Me?" Peter said "yes." Jesus then told him how to show that love, by feeding His lambs and sheep. Love is active. It is never just a feeling or emotion.

In Matthew 22:39 [AMPC] Jesus explains how we are to love: "You shall love your neighbor as [you do] yourself."

Healing, a Finished Work

Does God still do anything about healing today?

We know Jesus has completed all His redemptive work on the cross and has carried our sicknesses, pains, weakness, and distress.

Genesis declares that man and woman were made for DOMINION, not trouble. You have command over your own heart. Jesus said, "Let not your heart be troubled, neither let it be afraid." (John 14:27)

The first half of that verse says, "Peace I leave with you, my peace I give unto you: not as the world gives, give I unto you." Why is God's peace not like the world's peace?

God's peace is based on Jesus' finished work of redemption. He died for our sins and was raised for our justification. That is an absolute fact! The Hebrew word for peace is shalom which means "nothing missing, and nothing broken." God's peace holds the promise of restoration, not just resignation. The world's so-called "peace" is based on merely accepting your problems.

We don't accept problems; we submit to God. We submit to Christ, the Head of the church. We submit to the Holy Spirit Who seals our hearts for God and gives wisdom to us.

Even so, don't expect your life to be like a family movie! You will face challenges. Each time you confess a fault to God, each time you forgive someone, you release power into your own life. You become stronger and more in control, just like God wants you to be.

Each time you speak a scripture about healing, you are placing faith in Jesus' finished work.

Marvelous Memory

What does it mean to be diligent? The New Testament word translated "diligent" means "to hurry, to endeavor, to study."

In essence, it means to do something well and do it quickly. Memorization is important and cannot be emphasized too much!

Time must be spent in memorization because this is one of the specific "ways" God has instructed us to use in our pursuit of His wisdom.

Believers need to meditate on the word of God; it will help them solve problems and make judgments.

Proverbs 3

1. My son, forget not my law; but let thine heart keep my commandments:
2. For length of days, and long life, and peace, shall they add to thee.
3. Let not mercy and truth forsake thee: bind them about thy neck; write them upon the table of thine heart:
4. So shalt thou find favor and good understanding in the sight of God and man.
5. Trust in the LORD with all thine heart; and lean not unto thine own understanding.
6. In all thy ways acknowledge him, and he shall direct thy paths.

To "write the Word on the table of the heart" refers to memorization of the Word. The ability to memorize is a precious gift of God. How many churches encourage memorization? How many Christians practice it?

Children in Sunday School sometimes memorize and recite verses and learn definitions of difficult biblical terms. They are told to spend time studying the Bible in preparation for the next Sunday's lesson.

Joshua 1: 8 emphasizes the idea of meditating on the Word of God and connects this to success. It states directly that the believer makes his or her own way prosperous.

This book of the law shall not depart out of thy mouth; but thou shall meditate therein day and night, that thou mayest observe to do all that is written therein: for then thou shalt make thy way prosperous, and then thou shalt have good success. (Joshua 1:8)

See Yourself as Healed

Spiritually underdeveloped people can be caught in a "poor me" cycle. "Why did you say that to ME? Why did you look at ME that way?"

As long as you see yourself as sick and hurting you will continue to look for someone to help you, someone you can draw sympathy from.

This means you will be going over your problems again and again in a cycle that will feed itself. More sympathy will not help you. God's compassion will! Isaiah 26:3 says, "You will keep him in perfect peace, whose mind is stayed on You, because he trusts in You."

See yourself as healed. Jesus is your Great Physician, and He will prescribe good words for your mouth, words that will turn your life around like, "Let the weak say I am strong."

Let God Reinvent You

A toddler must learn to be a child; a child must learn to be a teen. A teen must learn to be an adult. Then comes college, the workplace, and marriage. Each life change requires a person to reinvent himself or herself over and over. Can we see this process in scripture? Yes!

David the shepherd boy killed a lion and a bear to protect the flock. Then, he killed Goliath and became a famous warrior. Later, he was a target for Saul's jealousy and became a leader of the discontented. Last of all, David became king.

You are always changing, but you are a spiritual being. True and lasting change must always proceed from the spirit, and it must be based on Christ's redemption.

He will alter the way you think. A troubled, worried, frustrated mind is an unrenewed mind.

If your family has taught you to be negative, you will have to break that tendency with the word of God. Repeating negative thoughts limits God's work on your behalf. Don't limit God like the Israelites did by speaking unbelief!

God has given you a sound mind, calm well-balanced thinking with discipline and self-control. Learn not to focus on what you feel.

Feelings are temporary; God's word is eternal.

The law of faith is found in Romans 10:8-10. With the heart man believes unto salvation: healing, peace, protection, provision, guidance, and strength.

With the mouth he confesses those things. What do you want your life to be like? God has a good life planned for you!

True Beauty

Isaiah 28:5-6 says:
In that day the LORD of hosts will be
For a crown of glory and a diadem of beauty
To the remnant of His people,
For a spirit of justice…and for strength.
He is our crown and our beauty! If we learn His ways our lives will be full of light!

Our lives should all be without spot or wrinkle, like a bride's dress. When I got married, I wore a borrowed gown, a leftover from my cousin's wedding. For me, that dress was perfect! It absolutely fit me like a glove. How could that be since it had been selected for another bride? For one thing, I had been dieting. For months I had said "no" to bread, pizza, and desserts. If I hadn't, that dress would not have fit me. If you learn to say "no" to hatred, bitterness, gossip, and all the works of the flesh, the life Jesus has planned for all believers will fit you perfectly!

In the midst of instructions about marriage, Paul gives precious insight about how Christ loved the church and gave Himself: "That he might sanctify and cleanse it with the washing of water by the word, that he might present it to himself a glorious church, not having spot, or wrinkle, or any such thing; but that it should be holy and without blemish." (Ephesians 5:27)

The Message translation says: "Christ's love makes the church whole. His words evoke her beauty. Everything he does and says is designed to bring the best out of her, dressing her in dazzling white silk, radiant with holiness."

This is what God wants for you, to "put on Christ," to be like Jesus. Galatians 3:27 (CEV) says, "And when you were baptized, it was as though you had put on Christ in the same way you put on new clothes."

You can see a progression in II Corinthians 6:6:

- ✓ By pureness – You refuse worldly thinking and embrace purity.
- ✓ By knowledge – Your knowledge of God's word grows.

- ✓ By longsuffering – You become more patient.
- ✓ By kindness – You become kinder to others.
- ✓ By the Holy Ghost – You yield to the Holy Spirit in a greater measure.
- ✓ By love unfeigned – Your love is based on truth, and it keeps growing!

He Will Speak to You!

When you begin to renew your mind and to shut out the world, you will hear Him more and more. This is not unusual. Jesus said, "My sheep know my voice." (John 10:27)

Isaiah 50:4 (GW) describes how God trains someone who wants to be His disciple: "The Almighty LORD will teach me what to say...Morning after morning he will wake me to listen like a student."

These verses, of course, refer to Jesus Christ, but we can also benefit from the wisdom contained in them. He will speak to you and open your spiritual ears to hear His voice. He will teach you how to talk and to take dominion with your words.

"With Me Where I AM"

John 17:24 (AMP) "Father, I desire that they also, whom You have given to Me [as Your gift to Me], may be with Me where I am, so that they may see My glory which You have given Me."

Where is Jesus now? John 14:2-3 says: "In my Father's house are many mansions: if it were not so, I would have told you. I go to prepare a place for you. And if I go and prepare a place for you, I will come again, and receive you unto myself; that where I am, there ye may be also."

Jesus will one day receive us to Himself, and where He is we shall be. We shall behold His glory in Heaven. Hebrews 8:1 says, "Now of the things which we have spoken this is the sum: We have such a high priest, who is set on the right hand of the throne of the Majesty in the heavens."

Jesus is seated at the right hand of the throne of God in the heavens. Jesus Christ also has a throne awaiting Him on the earth; it is the throne of His father David. At present, He is not on David's throne, although He will be.

Right now, He is sitting "upon the throne of His glory." (Matthew 25:31) If we overcome, we will sit with Him on His throne. Revelation 3:21 says, "To him that overcomes will I grant to sit with me in my throne, even as I also overcame, and am set down with my Father in his throne."

Conclusion

The statement "love never fails" is the summation of the New Testament as far as God is concerned. His love will never fail, and He expressed His love through Jesus Christ. The most Christlike way to live is to love others.

Stop seeing yourself as a victim! See God's love and Jesus' victory in your own life. You can be free because of Christ's victory; that is part of God's magnificent plan for you!

We cannot make ourselves holy. Jesus' blood contains all the holiness you need! You cannot open heaven's door. Without His blood, it will not open for you. No preacher, no priest, no evangelist can open it by themselves.

Jesus not only opens the door of heaven for those who believe on His name, He welcomes you into the very presence of God!

Jesus does the impossible. He sets at liberty those who are bruised. Jesus heals the hopelessly sick and scarred ones. He will heal you! Call upon the name of Jesus now!

"May grace (God's favor) and peace (which is perfect well-being, all necessary good, all spiritual prosperity, and freedom from fears and agitating passions and moral conflicts) be multiplied to you in [the full, personal, precise, and correct] knowledge of God and of Jesus our Lord." II Peter 1:2 (AMPC)

God sees you as perfect already because of your righteous standing in Christ. What does that mean? It means He has made you eligible to get every good thing God has. It means you are protected with armor that no anxiety can pierce. You have strength that no grief or rejection can overcome.

Your spirit is radiant with God's faith, hope, and love, and you truly are all glorious within! Psalm 90:1 - And let the beauty and delightfulness and favor of the Lord our God be upon us.

God's love is a supernatural force. It will never fail. Human love will always be limited by human strength. When human strength fails, their love will fail and disappoint you.

My story is a story of spiritual landmarks and a story of hope! His promises are true! God loves you with a never-ending love. His covenant love and loyalty are everlasting. Surrender to Jesus and be loved and restored!

Arise

[from the depression and prostration
in which circumstances have kept you
—rise to a new life]!
Shine
(be radiant with the glory of the Lord),
For your light has come,
and the glory of the Lord has risen upon you!
(Isaiah 60:1 AMPC)

An Outline for Recovery

1. Proverbs 2:6 - For the LORD gives wisdom; From His mouth *come* knowledge and understanding.

2. Proverbs 3:5 - Trust in the LORD with all your heart,
   And lean not on your own understanding.

3. Proverbs 3:7-8 - Fear the LORD and depart from evil. It will be health to your [c]flesh,
   And strength[d] to your bones.

4. Proverbs 3:11-12 - My son, do not despise the chastening of the LORD,
   Nor detest His correction; For whom the LORD loves He corrects,
   Just as a father the son *in whom* he delights.

5. Proverbs 3:25 - Do not be afraid of sudden terror,

6. Proverbs 3:27 - Do not withhold good from those to whom it is due,
When it is in the power of your hand to do *so.*

7. Proverbs 4:23 - Keep your heart with all diligence,
For out of it *spring* the issues of life.

Jean Vowell escaped depression by trusting in the wisdom of the Bible. She went from being housebound to being an honor student in college, and finally an instructor of college-level English classes. Jean used godly wisdom to teach and motivate students, encouraging them to go higher and farther than they ever dreamed they could.

Books:

Life, Liberty, and Leadership: Praying for Those in Authority

This book is not a study of American government or politics. It is not a comprehensive guide on how to pray. It is simply the story of how one family learned to honor God's word and to pray for our country's leaders.

Pedro's Navidad

This Christian young adult novel is about Pedro and his friends. Everything about Pedro's life was changing. He was finishing high school and making decisions about his future life. New friends, especially a retired pilot and a high school boy convicted of robbery, would take him in many new directions!

Ivan had been convicted of robbery and had run away. Now, Pedro set off to find his friend. It was almost Christmas Eve. Surely, Ivan had not ventured toward the old rope bridge!

Awake? Miss Church?

Has your family been out of church for a while? Ours had! This is the humorous and heartfelt story of how we found our way back to God, and to church!

Booklets:

Psalms for Soldiers

Psalms for Sailors

Prayers for Pilots

Psalms for Airmen

Psalms for Coast Guardsmen

Psalms for Marines

Psalms for Nurses

Psalms for Firefighters

Psalms for Law Enforcement Officers

www.ingramcontent.com/pod-product-compliance
Lightning Source LLC
LaVergne TN
LVHW012052160826
845678LV00014B/2796
9798842189656